JN412366

The
CHEONJEON-RI PETROGLYPHS
in Ulsan

Authors

Jeon Hotae
Professor, University of Ulsan

Jang Myeong-su
Director, Seokyeong Cultural Properties Research Institute

Gang Jong-hun
Professor, Catholic University of Daegu

Nam Yeon-ui
Researcher, Bangudae Petroglyphs Institute, University of Ulsan

Yoon Hyo-jeong
Researcher, Bangudae Petroglyphs Institute, University of Ulsan

Translator

Kim Jiyeon
Research Professor, University of Ulsan

Petroglyphs of Korea · I

The CHEONJEON-RI PETROGLYPHS in Ulsan

Bangudae Petroglyphs Institute, University of Ulsan

Hollym

The Cheonjeon-ri Petroglyphs in Ulsan

First edition, 2014
by Hollym International Corp., USA
Phone 908 353 1655 **Fax** 908 353 0255
http://www.hollym.com **e-Mail** contact@hollym.com

Published simultaneously in Korea
by Hollym Corp., Publishers, Seoul, Korea
Phone +82 2 734 5087 **Fax** +82 2 730 5149
http://www.hollym.co.kr **e-Mail** info@hollym.co.kr

ISBN: 978-1-56591-411-7
Library of Congress Control Number: 2014945000

Printed in Korea

Contents

Tables

Photos

Figures

Preface

The collection of engraved stones at Cheonjeon-ri is not only a work of art but also a historical document that contains various historic and cultural sources ranging from prehistoric petroglyphs to inscriptions dating from the Three Kingdoms (1st century BCE-7th century CE) and the Unified Silla periods (668-935 CE). The site, which was discovered by a Dongguk University research team on December 25, 1970, is the first petroglyph site found on the Korean peninsula. The Cheonjeon-ri Petroglyphs consist of a large rectangular rock panel under a low hill, and several other rocks located north of this main panel.

The Daegok Stream flows in front of the Cheonjeon-ri stone panels and across the stream on the other side stands a high rock cliff, about 2 kilometers from the Bangudae Petroglyphs, another major petroglyph site. Below the high cliff lie large rock beds that reach all the way down to the Daegok Stream and are punctuated by about 200 dinosaur footprints from the Cretaceous period, most of them longer than 30 centimeters.

The main panel faces east and leans slightly forward toward the stream. Therefore, the sun hits the rock face only for a limited time during the day, which is the only time that the petroglyphs can be observed. The main panel is 9.5 meters wide and 2.7 meters tall. The other rock panels range in width and height from 1 meter to 2.5 meters.

Numerous figures of deer, dogs, unidentifiable animals, human faces, full-length human bodies, and geometric patterns are carved on the main panel. Procession scenes, boats, and mystic animals are engraved with thin lines, and there are more than 1,000 inscribed letters. Various interpretations of these figures and textual inscriptions have been presented since the discovery of the site, but none of them are widely accepted by specialists or the public. There are several reasons for the lack of more profound research and analysis of this site, including the complexity of the contents and the lack of researchers specializing in petroglyphs. The absence of resources based on accurate surveys is at the root of the dearth of research.

Considering this situation, I believe that *The Cheonjeon-ri Petroglyphs in Ulsan* published by the Bangudae Institute of the University of Ulsan is a great step forward in the study of this important site, an accomplishment that should be recognized by scholars both in and outside Korea studying rock art sites, ancient texts, and other historic relics. In fact, several survey reports of the site have been made, focusing on figures or inscriptions or on particular works or techniques, depending on the interests of the researchers. However, an analysis, categorization and cataloguing of all the carvings have not been done.

The publication of *The Cheonjeon-ri Petroglyphs in Ulsan* was the first project that I implemented as the director of the Bangudae Institute. I first reviewed the previous research of the site and studied possible methods that could be used to categorize and number the carvings. During this process, Dr. Jang Myeong-su, the director of the Seokyeong Research Institute of Cultural Property, offered illustrations of the site based on the tracing of the life-size replica and inscriptions he had collected for more than ten years. In addition, Professor Gang Jong-hun of the Catholic University of Daegu took on the task of doing an in-depth analysis of the inscriptions. Two researchers with the Bangudae Institute, Nam Yeon-ui and Yoon Hyo-jeong, categorized the figures and organized the sources. The publication of this report would not have been possible without the help of these people. I extend my sincere gratitude to all of them.

Jeon Hotae

Director, Bangudae Petroglyphs Institute, University of Ulsan

January, 2014

Photo 1. Satellite photograph of the Cheonjeon-ri Petroglyphs and surrounding area (credit: http://maps.google.co.kr)

Location of the Site and Environment

1. Natural and Geological Environment

The Cheonjeon-ri Petroglyphs of Ulsan is part of the Daegok Stream Petroglyphs carved on the cliffs standing alongside the Daegok Stream. The steep cliffs containing the petroglyphs were formed by continuous erosion caused by the stream that winds through the Daegok Valley for several kilometers.

The Cheonjeon-ri Petroglyphs are located at San 210, Cheonjeon-ri, Dudong-myeon, Ulju-gun, Ulsan Metropolitan City, and latitude 35° 36' 52" north, longitude 129° 10' 29" east. The Daegok Stream flows right in front of the rock panels. The petroglyphs were first discovered on December 25, 1970 by a Dongguk University research team who were surveying the Buddhist relics in the region. The site was designated National Treasure No. 147 in 1973 and it has been protected as such ever since. The high cliff facing the Cheonjeon-ri Petroglyphs on the other side of the stream stretches to Daegok-ri, where the Bangudae Petroglyphs (National Treasure No. 285) are located, 1.2 kilometers away.

The Daegok Stream starts from the Gaji Mountain (1,240 m above sea level) and flows into the Taehwa River around Gogyeon Village of the Ulsan Metropolitan City, which is about 26 kilometers from Ulsan Bay. The stream forms "incised meanders" that created the deep valley around the Mesozoic sedimentary rock areas of Cheonjeon-ri and Bangudae.[1]

1 "Incised meander" means a river meander that has been cut deeply into the river as the river is newly eroded by the uplift of the land. These meanders, which demonstrate that the land of the Korean peninsula has been uplifted, appear in deep valleys located at the upper streams of the rivers, creating beautiful surrounding landscapes. For the geological formation and environmental changes around the Taehwa River regions, see Hwang S. and Yun S. 2000: 67-112.

On the east side of the Daegok Dam stands Yeonhwa Mountain (532 m above sea level), which divides Eunpyeon-ri of Dudong-myeon township and Daegok-myeon township. Another mountain, Guksubong (620 m above sea level), is located between the Dudong-myeon and Beomseo-myeon townships of Ulju-gun. Mabyeong Mountain (511 m above sea level) is on the west, and Ami Mountain (601 m above sea level) and Yongam Mountain (589 m above sea level) stand on the northwest side of Duseo-myeon township. The Daegok Stream, which is also called Bangu Stream, is formed with water flowing from all these mountains.

The soil around Bangudae belongs to the lower layers of the Gyeongsang supergroup of Mesozoic sedimentary deposits. The rocks around the Cheonjeon-ri panels can be categorized as gray sandy mudstone layers of the Sayeon-ri layer, which belongs to the Cretaceous Daegu Layer, a lower layer of Gyeongsang supergroup (Korean Institute of Geoscience and Mineral Resources 1972).

There are more than 200 dinosaur footprints on the flat rock beds in front of the Cheonjeon-ri Petroglyphs. Most of them belong to medium to large size plant eaters. Footprints of various kinds of dinosaurs have also been found around the Bangudae Petroglyphs, and new ones were identified through recent excavations. Clearly, the Daegok Stream area was a dinosaur habitat of the Mesozoic period.

Fig. 1. Location of the Cheonjeon-ri Petroglyphs and topography around the area

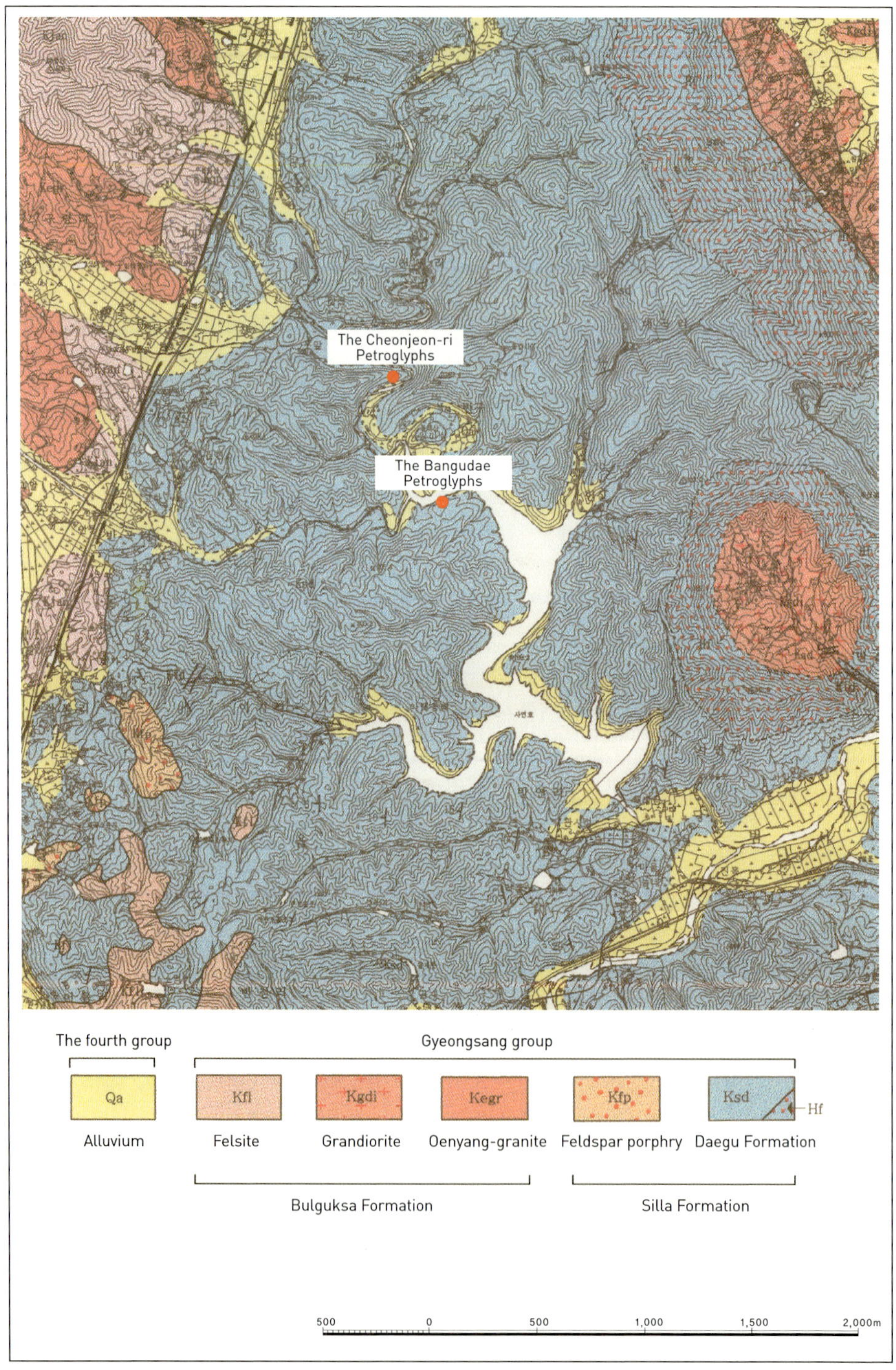

Fig. 2. Geological map around the Cheonjeon-ri Petroglyphs

2. Archeological and Historical Environment

The landscape around the middle and upper reaches of the Daegok Stream is characterized by deep valleys, meandering rivers, overlapping mountains, and soaring rocks, a beautiful land formation created by incised meanders. Because of the scenic beauty of the area, many poets and literati visited here during the Three Kingdoms, Goryeo (918-1392), and Joseon (1392-1910) periods; they composed poems, painted pictures, and enjoyed wine and music (Seong B. 2010). Such activities are recorded in numerous texts, and the inscriptions on the Cheonjeon-ri rock panel are an important part of these records.

Many other relics and historic sites from different periods are found in the Bangudae and Cheonjeon-ri areas, because the low hills of the upper reaches of the Daegok Stream provided a good environment for settlers. The relics range from Bronze Age dwellings to Goryeo and Joseon tombs and pottery kilns. During the construction of the Daegok Dam in 2003, some Bronze Age dwelling sites and tombs were found in Hasamjeong of Samjeong-ri, Ulju, which yielded more than 1,000 artifacts including wooden casket tombs of the Three Hans period and wooden casket tombs, jar burial tombs, and stone mound tombs of the Three Kingdoms period. Pottery shards of the Three Kingdoms period were also excavated up on of the hill where the Cheonjeon-ri Petroglyphs are located, and the site of Bango-sa, a Unified Silla temple, was found on the northern slope of the hill across the Daegok Stream.

Fig. 3. Relic sites around the Cheonjeon-ri Petroglyphs

Relic sites around Daegok Stream where the Cheonjeon-ri Petroglyphs are located and their characteristics are as follows:

Table 1. Distribution of relics around the Cheonjeon-ri and the Daegok Stream

Number	Name of the site	Period	Characteristics of the site	Bibliography	Survey type
1	Cheonjeon-ri Relic Site, Ulju-gun	Three Kingdoms period	Location: Hills around the Choenjeon-ri. Relics: Three Kingdoms period relics including poetry shards were found. Presumably Three Kingdoms period tombs and dwelling sites.	Ulsan Metropolitan City, 2003. *Munhwa yujeok bunpo jido: Ulju-gun.*	Surface
2	Bango-sa Temple Site, Ulju-gun	Unified Silla	Location: North of Chenjeon-ri. Relics: Scattered pieces of roof stones and body stones. The body is now in the Busan University Museum.	Ulsan Metropolitan City, 2003. *Munhwa yujeok bunpo jido: Ulju-gun.*	Surface
3	Daegok-ri Relic Sites, Ulju-gun	Joseon period	Location: North of Bangu Village. Relics: Porcelain shards and earthen ware shards from the Joseon period. Presumably Joseon period tombs and dwelling sites.	Ulsan Metropolitan City, 2003. *Munhwa yujeok bunpo jido: Ulju-gun.*	Surface
4	Dongmaesil Relic Sites, Daegok-ri, Ulju-gun	Joseon period	Location: Dongmaesil, north of Bangu Village. Relics: Porcelain shards and earthen ware shards from the Joseon period. Presumably Joseon period tombs and dwelling sites.	Ulsan Metropolitan City, 2003. *Munhwa yujeok bunpo jido: Ulju-gun.*	Surface
5	Bangudae Relic Sites, Daegok-ri, Ulju-gun	Joseon period	Location: At the end of the west side of the hill standing north of the Bangudae Petroglyphs. Relics: Tile kilns and tiles from the Joseon period. Presumably Joseon kiln and dwelling sites.	Ulsan Metropolitan City, 2003. *Munhwa yujeok bunpo jido: Ulju-gun.*	Surface
6	Bangudae Petroglyphs, Daegok-ri, Ulju-gun	Neolithic to Bronze Age	National Treasure No.285. Various petroglyphs at the lower part of a cliff. More than ten panels containing petroglyphs. The width of the main panel is 8m and the height is 4m. 81 dinosaur footprints from the Cretaceous period found on the rock beds beneath the Bangudae rock panels. Ever since the Sayeon Dam was built in 1965, the rock panels the rock panels became submerged most of the year, and are only exposed during the dry season. Currently, the Ulsan Metropolitan City and the Cultural Administration of Korea are discussing and negotiating on the possible method of the site's preservation	Excavation by National Research Institute of Cultural Heritage: Aug. 30, 2013 – Nov. 30, 2013. Hwang S. and Mun M, 1984. *Bangudae ambyeokjogak*, Dongguk University. National Research Institute of Cultural Heritage, 2011. *Bangudae ambyeokjogak.* Ulsan Petroglyphs Museum, 2013. *Hangukui amgakhwa III, Ulju Daegok-ri Bangudae amgakhwa.* University of Ulsan Museum, 2000. *Ulsan Bangudae amgakhwa.*	Cultural property research

Num ber	Name of the site	Period	Characteristics of the site	Bibliography	Survey type
7	Daegok-ri Bangu Seowon Relic Sites, Ulju-gun	Goryeo period	Location: Southern side of the hill west of Bangu Seowon (Confucian academy). Relics: Celadon, porcelain, and earthen ware shards. Presumably Goryeo and Joseon buildings and dwelling sites.	Ulsan Metropolitan City, 2003. *Munhwa yujeok bunpo jido: Ulju-gun.*	Surface
8	Apgol Kiln Site 3, Cheonjeon-ri, Ulju-gun	Joseon period	Subterranean flat kiln. The length of the kiln is 690cm. width 250cm. depth 72cm. Production of coals from the Joseon period.	Ulsan Research Institute of Cultural Property, 2005. *Ulsan Cheonjeon-ri Jinhyeon, Apgol yujeok.*	Excavation
9	Apgol Kiln Site 2, Cheonjeon-ri, Ulju-gun	Goryeo period	Part of the firing room was discovered. Based on the pottery shards found inside, the kiln was used between the mid-13th century and the late-14th century.	Ulsan Research Institute of Cultural Property, 2005. *Ulsan Cheonjeon-ri Jinhyeon, Apgol yujeok.*	Excavation
10	Apgol Kiln Site 1, Cheonjeon-ri, Ulju-gun	Unified Silla	Part of the firing room was discovered. Subterranean flat kiln. Based on the stamped pattern on the pottery shards, the kiln was used between the mid-7th century and the early 8th century.	Ulsan Research Institute of Cultural Property, 2005. *Ulsan Cheonjeon-ri Jinhyeon, Apgol yujeok.*	Excavation
11	Jinhyeon Site, Cheonjeon-ri, Ulju-gun	Bronze Age	Two dwelling sites of presumably four pillar type. Based on the type of pottery found inside the house, the site is dated to the Bronze Age.	Ulsan Research Institute of Cultural Property, 2005. *Ulsan Cheonjeon-ri Jinhyeon, Apgol yujeok.*	Excavation
12	Witjinti Site, Cheonjeon-ri, Ulju-gun	Unified Silla	Location: Eastern hill of the Witjinti Village. Relics: Pottery shards from the Unified Silla through the Joseon period. Presumably Unified Silla tombs and dwelling sites.	Ulsan Metropolitan City, 2003. *Munhwa yujeok bunpo jido: Ulju-gun.*	Surface
13	Araetjinti Site, Cheonjeon-ri, Ulju-gun	Bronze Age	Location: The hill across the Witjinti Site. Relics: Ground stone axes, hard and soft earthen ware shards. Presumably dwelling sites of the Bronze Age and the Three Kingdoms period.	Ulsan Metropolitan City, 2003. *Munhwa yujeok bunpo jido: Ulju-gun.*	Surface
14	Goha Tomb Site, Bangok-ri, Ulju-gun	Three Kingdoms period	Location: Goha Valley, east of Goha Village. Relics: Broken stone coffins, long-neck jars, and short-neck jars. Based on the types of relics, the tomb site is dated to the Three Kingdoms period.	Ulsan Metropolitan City, 2003. *Munhwa yujeok bunpo jido: Ulju-gun.*	Surface
15	Bangok-cheon Relic Site, Bangok-ri, Ulju-gun	Three Kingdoms period	Location: East of Goha Tomb site. Relics: Earthen ware, porcelain, and Buncheong ware shards. Mixture of Three Kingdoms and Joseon period tombs and dwelling sites.	Ulsan Metropolitan City, 2003. *Munhwa yujeok bunpo jido: Ulju-gun.*	Surface

Number	Name of the site	Period	Characteristics of the site	Bibliography	Survey type
16	Amgol Relic Site, Daegok-ri, Ulju-gun	Unified Silla	Location: Amgol, north of Hansil Village. Relics: Long neck jars with dish-shaped mouth. Presumably Unified Silla tombs.	Ulsan Metropolitan City, 2003. *Munhwa yujeok bunpo jido: Ulju-gun.*	Surface
17	Hansil Relic Site, Daegok-ri, Ulju-gun	Joseon period	Location: East of Goha Tomb site. Relics: Earthen ware, porcelain, and Buncheong ware shards. Presumably Joseon tombs and dwelling sites.	Ulsan Metropolitan City, 2003. *Munhwa yujeok bunpo jido: Ulju-gun.*	Surface
18	Cheonjeon-ri Site, Ulju-gun	Joseon period	Location: Northwest side of Cheonjeon Village. Relics: No particular relics found except modern waterways.	Central Institute of Cultural Heritage, 2004. *Gukdo 35 hoseon hawk pojang gongsa gugannae balguljosa bogoseo.*	Excavation
19	Cheonjeon-ri Tomb Site, Ulju-gun	Three Kingdoms period	Location: Northwest of Daehyeon Village. Relics: More than ten tumuli of 5-7 meters in diameter. Earthen ware shards from the Three Kingdoms period.	Ulsan Metropolitan City, 2003. *Munhwa yujeok bunpo jido: Ulju-gun.*	Surface
20	Seodang Kiln Site, Cheonjeon-ri, Ulju-gun	Joseon period	Location: North of Daehyeon Village. Relics: Pottery shards and broken kiln parts.	Ulsan Metropolitan City, 2003. *Munhwa yujeok bunpo jido: Ulju-gun.*	Surface
21	Guksarim Relic Site, Cheonjeon-ri, Ulju-gun	Joseon period	Location: Northeast of Jangcheon Village. Relics: Buncheong ware, porcelain, and earthen ware shards. Presumably Joseon tombs and dwelling sites.	Ulsan Metropolitan City, 2003. *Munhwa yujeok bunpo jido: Ulju-gun.*	Surface
22	Jangcheon-sa Temple Site, Cheonjeon-ri, Ulju-gun	Unified Silla	Location: East of Guksarim Archaeological Site. Relics: Remains of the temple including five buildings, two walls, ten waterways, two terraces. Roof tile with the inscription, "Jangcheon-sa Temple."	Korea Cultural Heritage Foundation, 2008. *Ulsan Hwalcheol, Seoha, Cheonjeon-ri yujeok.*	Excavation
23	Cheonjeon-ri Site, Ulju-gun	Joseon period	Location: South of Bang-ri iron production site. Relics: Ten reclining kilns, one jar kiln, and others.	Korea Cultural Heritage Foundation, 2008. *Ulsan Hwalcheol, Seoha, Cheonjeon-ri yujeok.*	Excavation
24	Bang-ri Iron Production Site, Cheonjeon-ri, Ulju-gun	Joseon period	Location: Inside the areas submerged with the construction of Daegok Dam. Relics: Two smelting sites, two firing sites, and others.	Korea Cultural Heritage Foundation, 2004. *Ulsangwon gwangyeok sangsudo (Daegok Dam) saeop pyeonip bujinae 2 cha balguljosa Ulsan Cheonjeon-ri, Bang-ri, Gojipyeong yujeok.*	Excavation

Num ber	Name of the site	Period	Characteristics of the site	Bibliography	Survey type
25	Bang-ri Temple Site, Cheonjeon-ri, Ulju-gun	Unified Silla	Relics: Temple remains including six buildings, four walls, and two waterways. Based on the excavated relics, a temple existed from the Unified Silla period through the Joseon period.	Korea Cultural Heritage Foundation, 2004. *Ulsangwon gwangyeok sangsudo (Daegok Dam) saeop pyeonip bujinae 2 cha balguljosa Ulsan Cheonjeon-ri, Bang-ri, Gojipyeong yujeok.*	Excavation
26	Bang-ri Site, Cheonjeon-ri, Ulju-gun	Unified Silla	Location: At the foot of the hill in Bang-ri Village. Relics: Two building sites, three waterway sites, and four kiln sites from the Unified Silla period, two building sites from the Joseon period, and others.	Korea Cultural Heritage Foundation, 2004. *Ulsangwon gwangyeok sangsudo (Daegok Dam) saeop pyeonip bujinae 2 cha balguljosa Ulsan Cheonjeon-ri, Bang-ri, Gojipyeong yujeok.*	Excavation
27	Gojipyeong Kiln Site, Cheonjeon-ri, Ulju-gun	Joseon period	Location: At the foot of the hill northeast of the Bang-ri Village. Relics: Three kilns, and one deposit site, and others. Joseon period porcelain kiln.	Korea Cultural Heritage Foundation, 2004. *Ulsangwon gwangyeok sangsudo (Daegok Dam) saeop pyeonip bujinae 2 cha balguljosa Ulsan Cheonjeon-ri, Bang-ri, Gojipyeong yujeok.*	Excavation
28	Seoha Site, Ulju-gun	Bronze Age	Relics: Six Bronze Age dwelling sites and earthen wares.	Korea Cultural Heritage Foundation, 2008. *Ulsan Hwalcheol, Seoha, Cheonjeon-ri yujeok.*	Excavation
29	Seoha-ri Apdeul Site, Ulju-gun	Bronze Age	Location: Eastern field of Seoha Village. Relics: Five Bronze Age dwelling sites and earthenwares.	Central Institute of Cultural Heritage, 2004. *Gukdo 35 hoseon hawk pojang gongsa gugannae balguljosa bogoseo.*	Excavation
30	Seoha-ri Tomb Site, Ulju-gun	Three Kingdoms period	Location: South of Seoha Village. Relics: Stones used for a stone coffin, earthen ware shards from the Three Kingdoms period.	Ulsan Metropolitan City, 2003. *Munhwa yujeok bunpo jido: Ulju-gun.*	Surface
31	Daejeong Relic Site, Seoha-ri, Ulju-gun	Three Kingdoms period	Location: West of Seoha Village. Relics: Earthen ware and porcelain shards from the Three Kingdoms period and the Joseon period. Presumably Three Kingdoms and Joseon tombs and dwelling sites.	Ulsan Metropolitan City, 2003. *Munhwa yujeok bunpo jido: Ulju-gun.*	Surface
32	Deokgeo Relic Site, Inbo-ri, Ulju-gun	Joseon period	Location: North of Inbo. Relics: Porcelain shards. Presumably Joseon period tombs and dwelling sites.	Ulsan Metropolitan City, 2003. *Munhwa yujeok bunpo jido: Ulju-gun.*	Surface

Num ber	Name of the site	Period	Characteristics of the site	Bibliography	Survey type
33	Hasamjeong Tomb Site, Samjeong-ri, Ulju-gun	Three Kingdoms period	Location: Hasamjeong Village. Relics: Wooden coffin tombs and wooden chamber and stone mound tombs from the Three Kingdoms period. Over 1,000 relics dated to 3th to 6th century.	Korea Cultural Heritage Foundation, 2009. *Ulsangwon gwangyeok sangsudo (Daegok Dam) saeop bujinae 4 cha balguljosa, Ulsan Hasamjeong gobungun I.* Korea Cultural Heritage Foundation, 2010. *Ulsangwon gwangyeok sangsudo (Daegok Dam) saeop bujinae 4 cha balguljosa, Ulsan Hasamjeong gobungun II.* Korea Cultural Heritage Foundation, 2011. *Ulsangwon gwangyeok sangsudo (Daegok Dam) saeop bujinae 4 cha balguljosa, Ulsan Hasamjeong gobungun III.* Korea Cultural Heritage Foundation, 2011. *Ulsangwon gwangyeok sangsudo (Daegok Dam) saeop bujinae 4 cha balguljosa, Ulsan Hasamjeong gobungun IV.* Korea Cultural Heritage Foundation, 2012. *Ulsangwon gwangyeok sangsudo (Daegok Dam) saeop bujinae 4 cha balguljosa, Ulsan Hasamjeong gobungun V.*	Excavation
34	Hasamjeong Site, Samjeong-ri, Ulju-gun	Samhan period	Location: Eastern hill of the Hasamjeong Village Relics: 108 relics including 1 Bronze Age dwelling site, 4 Three Kingdoms wooden coffin tombs, 3 jar burial pits, and 29 wooden coffin tombs.	Korea Cultural Heritage Foundation, 2007. *Ulsangwon gwangyeok sangsudo (Daegok Dam) saeop pyeonip bujinae 3 cha balguljosa, Ulsan Hasamjeong yujeok, bang-rionggi yujeok.*	Excavation
35	Samjeong-ri Site, Ulju-gun	Joseon period	Relics: Plain pottery shards from the Bronze Age.	Korea Cultural Heritage Foundation, 2008. *Ulsangwon gwangyeok sangsudo (Daegok Dam) saeop bujinae 5 cha balguljosa, Ulsan Daemil, Yangsujeon, Sangsamjeong, Samjeong-ri yujeok.*	Excavation
36	Taegi-ri Relic Site, Ulju-gun	Joseon period	Location: Northern Hill of Taegi-ri. Relics: Porcelain and earthen ware shards. Presumably Joseon period tombs and dwelling sites.	Ulsan Metropolitan City, 2003. *Munhwa yujeok bunpo jido: Ulju-gun.*	Surface
37	Taegi-ri Kiln Site, Ulju-gun	Joseon period	Location: Valley at the end of Sayeon Dam. Relics: Porcelain and Buncheong ware shards. Presumably Joseon period kiln site.	Ulsan Metropolitan City, 2003. *Munhwa yujeok bunpo jido: Ulju-gun.*	Surface
38	Dinosaur footprints, Cheonjeon-ri, Ulju-gun	Cretaceous period	Location: Rock beds across the Cheonjeon-ri Petroglyphs. Relics: Over 200 dinosaur footprints from the Cretaceous period. The lengths are between 20cm and 70cm, and the strides are between 120cm and 170cm. Mid to large size plant eaters such as Ultrasaurus.	Ulsan Metropolitan City. *Munhwa jaryo 6.*	Cultural property

Number	Name of the site	Period	Characteristics of the site	Bibliography	Survey type
39	Dinosaur footprints, Daegok-ri, Ulju-gun	Cretaceous period	Location: Rock beds across the Cheonjeon-ri Petroglyphs. Relics: About 13 dinosaur footprints from the Cretaceous period. The lengths are between 74cm and 76cm, and the depths are between 7cm and 10cm.	Ulsan Metropolitan City. *Munhwa jaryo 13.*	Cultural property

The Cheonjeon-ri Petroglyphs are located in Dudong-myeon township, which was part of Goheo-bu, one of the Six Districts of Silla. It was renamed Saryang-bu in 32 BCE (32nd year of the reign of King Yuri of Silla) and again to Namsan-bu in 940 (23rd year of the reign of King Taejo of Goryeo). Guryangbeol and Madeungo were incorporated into this district. Later it became Nam-myeon, and again Oenam-myeon (outer Nam-myeon) during the reign of King Jeongjo in the 18th century. In 1905, it was again renamed, Dubuk-myeon, and made a sub-district of Ulsan-gun. The meaning of *dubuk* is "north of Big Deeper," indicating that the area was located north of a village. In 1917, Dubok-myeon was divided into Dudong-myeon (East Du) and Duseo-myeon (West Du) across the road that connects Gyeongju and Eonyang.

Cheonjeon-ri was called Najeon when it belonged to Nam-myeon, but in 1911, it was renamed Cheonjeon, and made a part of Dubuk-myeon. In 1913, Cheonjeon and part of Bangok-ri were merged and designated a new district, Cheonjeon-ri. Both Naejeon and Cheonjeon mean "village in front of a stream."

Classification of Images

The Cheonjeon-ri Petroglyphs are carved on a large rock panel 2.7 meters high and 9.5 meters wide and on several other smaller panels, located on the right side of the main rock panel. The large rock panel is facing southeast, toward the Daegok Stream, and leans slightly forward, about 15 degrees.

Table 2. Classification of individual figures of the Cheonjeon-ri Petroglyphs

Rock Panels / Types of figures		Panel A				Panel B	Panel C	Panel D	Total
		I	II	TLE	TI				
Humans	Full body / Lower body	3	9	22					34
	Face	1	1						2
	Mounted figures			23				2	25
Animals	Artiodactyla	93	1	27					121
	Carnivora	26				2			28
	Fish / Other animals	6							6
	Birds			2					2
	Dragons			4					4
	Unidentified	55		2		8			65
Geometric patterns	Lozenges		42					1	43
	Circles		29					1	30
	Waves		10					2	12
	Check patterns						1		1
	Unidentified		5				2		7
Text	Textual inscriptions				218				218
	Modern inscriptions				3	3	11	18	35

Types of figures \ Rock Panels	Panel A				Panel B	Panel C	Panel D	Total
	I	II	TLE	TI				
Tools	1		2					3
Man-made structures			18					18
Plants	1		14				1	16
Unidentified	31	38	13		5	14	6	107
Total	217	135	127	221	18	28	31	777

Here, the main rock is called Panel A, and the others are referred to as Panel B, C, and D (refer to Photo 4). It is very difficult to identify individual figures carved on these rock panels as most figures are crowded in groups and connected to each other. Identifying geometric patterns is especially difficult. This difficulty was pointed out by a previous report, which argued that individual identification of figures could interfere with understanding the real meaning of the petroglyphs in their entirety (KRIPA 2003). Nonetheless, the following is an attempt to provide illustrations of individual figures in order to provide primary sources for future research. The images are grouped by panel, and then by the category or type. The size of the figures are based on the S=1:20 scale.

777 individual figures have been identified, including 253 textual inscriptions (32%), 226 animals (29%), 93 geometric patterns (12%), 61 human figures (8%), 21 tools and man-made structures (3%), and 16 plants (2%). Among the inscriptions, 221 are located on the lower section of Panel A and 32 are modern inscriptions located on Panels B, C, and D.

Photo 2. The Cheonjeon-ri Petroglyphs Site and its vicinities

Photo 3. A complete view of the Cheonjeon-ri Petroglyphs

Photo 4. Location of rock panels, the Cheonjeon-ri Petroglyphs (Panel A-D)

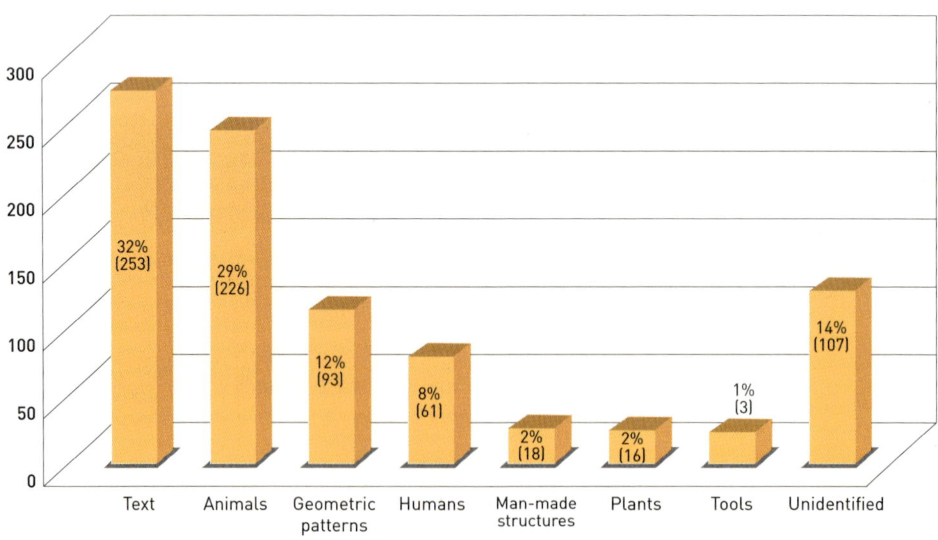

Fig. 4. Distribution of figure types (Panel A-D)

Photo 5. A complete view of panel A, the Cheonjeon-ri Petroglyphs

Photo 6. Panel A, the Cheonjeon-ri Petroglyphs

1. Panel A

There are numerous traces of chipping, but these traces cannot be recognized as identifiable patterns or structures. Besides these traces, the rest of the engravings are categorized based on the types of figures. Layers of figures are engraved on Panel A, each featuring a different technique, subject, and style. The upper part of the main panel is engraved mostly with geometric patterns. Various animal silhouettes created by shallow chipping are visible beneath these geometric patterns. Figures engraved in thin lines and textual inscriptions are found on the lower part of the main panel. This panel has attracted great attention as it displays layers of different types of figures and inscriptions produced over a long period of time, which explains the variety and complexity of this site.

The earliest among them are animal silhouettes in shallow chipping (A-I). The geometric images made with chipping and grinding are thought to be have been produced next (A-II). Finally, the detailed line drawings (A-TLE) and inscriptions, engraved on the lower section of the panel, were produced.

"Chipping" can be divided into three types—deep, medium, and shallow chipping. Each type is indicated by a different color. The geometric patterns appear to have been chipped first and deepened by grinding.

Thin line engraving was used for procession scenes (A-TLE-24, 25, 27, 33, 34, 35, 36), boats (40, 41), dragons (42, 115) and for inscriptions. Figures engraved with these techniques are located mostly on the lower part of the panel. Chipping was partly used to erase or modify previously engraved figures. In the case of A-TI-43, 56, 118, 157, the characters were engraved by chipping only.

Of the 777 figures comprising the Cheonjeon-ri Petroglyphs, 700 are on Panel A (A-I: 217, A-II: 135, A-TLE: 127, A-TI: 221). Inscriptions account for 32% (221) of all the engravings. Detailed depictions of animals engraved with thin lines (A-TLE) and silhouettes of animals created by chipping (A-I) account for 31% (216) of the petroglyphs, geometric patterns (A-II) 12% (86), human figures 8% (59), tools and man-made structures 3% (21), and plants 2% (15). There are 82 unidentified images, which account for 12% of the all the petroglyphs.

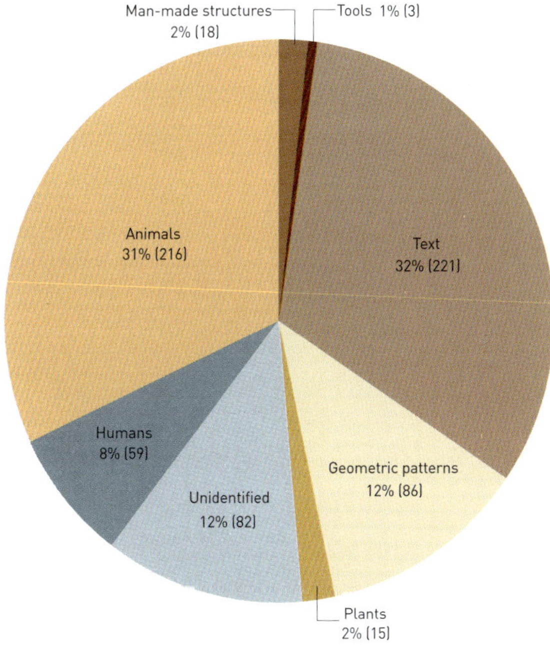

Fig. 5. Distribution of figure types (Panel A)

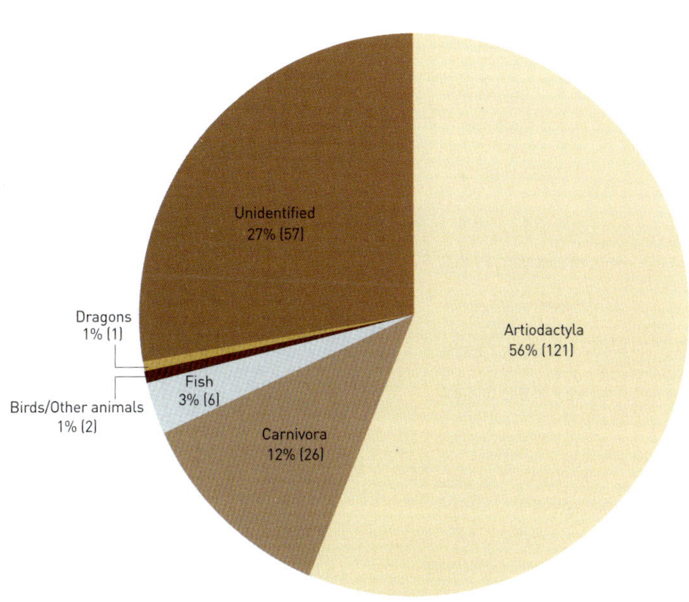

Fig. 6. Distribution of animal figures (Panel A)

Table 3. Classification of individual figures (A-I)

Number	Group	Type	Length (mm)	Height (mm)	Carving technique
A-I-1	Animals	Artiodactyla / Cervidae	760	220	Silhouette chipping
A-I-2	Animals	Artiodactyla / Cervidae	480	260	Silhouette chipping
A-I-3	Animals	Artiodactyla / Cervidae	480	180	Silhouette chipping
A-I-4	Animals	Carnivora / Felidae	270	340	Silhouette chipping
A-I-5	Animals	Unidentified	220	80	Silhouette chipping
A-I-6	Animals	Unidentified	220	220	Silhouette chipping
A-I-7	Animals	Carnivora / Felidae	420	150	Silhouette chipping
A-I-8	Animals	Artiodactyla	240	200	Silhouette chipping
A-I-9	Animals	Artiodactyla / Cervidae	430	460	Silhouette chipping
A-I-10	Animals	Artiodactyla / Cervidae	20	380	Silhouette chipping
A-I-11	Animals	Carnivora / Felidae	420	200	Silhouette chipping
A-I-12	Animals	Artiodactyla / Cervidae	430	460	Silhouette chipping
A-I-13	Animals	Artiodactyla / Cervidae	560	260	Silhouette chipping
A-I-14	Humans	Full body	320	580	Silhouette chipping
A-I-15	Tools	Bow	320	280	Silhouette chipping
A-I-16	Animals	Artiodactyla / Cervidae	200	140	Silhouette chipping
A-I-17	Animals	Artiodactyla / Cervidae	260	240	Silhouette chipping
A-I-18	Animals	Carnivora / Felidae	260	120	Silhouette chipping
A-I-19-1	Animals	Carnivora / Felidae	356	520	Silhouette chipping
A-I-19-2	Humans	Face	180	260	Silhouette chipping
A-I-20	Humans	Full body	450	440	Silhouette chipping
A-I-21	Animals	Artiodactyla / Cervidae	360	440	Silhouette chipping
A-I-22	Animals	Artiodactyla / Cervidae	460	640	Silhouette chipping
A-I-23	Animals	Artiodactyla / Cervidae	480	430	Silhouette chipping
A-I-24	Animals	Artiodactyla / Cervidae	480	430	Silhouette chipping
A-I-25	Animals	Artiodactyla / Cervidae	200	140	Silhouette chipping
A-I-26	Animals	Artiodactyla / Cervidae	340	180	Silhouette chipping
A-I-27	Animals	Artiodactyla / Cervidae	340	200	Silhouette chipping
A-I-28	Animals	Artiodactyla / Cervidae	200	220	Silhouette chipping
A-I-29	Animals	Artiodactyla / Unidentified	620	480	Silhouette chipping
A-I-30	Unidentified	Unidentified	360	160	Silhouette chipping
A-I-31	Animals	Artiodactyla / Cervidae	200	120	Silhouette chipping

Number	Group	Type	Length (mm)	Height (mm)	Carving technique
A-I-32	Animals	Artiodactyla / Cervidae	360	320	Silhouette chipping
A-I-33	Animals	Unidentified	300	200	Silhouette chipping
A-I-34	Animals	Artiodactyla / Bovidae	460	260	Silhouette chipping
A-I-35	Animals	Unidentified	220	100	Silhouette chipping
A-I-36	Unidentified	Unidentified	260	20	Silhouette chipping
A-I-37	Animals	Unidentified	520	460	Silhouette chipping
A-I-38	Animals	Unidentified	80	240	Silhouette chipping
A-I-39	Animals	Artiodactyla / Suideos	240	140	Silhouette chipping
A-I-40	Unidentified	Unidentified	420	100	Silhouette chipping
A-I-41	Animals	Unidentified	250	180	Silhouette chipping
A-I-42	Animals	Unidentified	280	230	Silhouette chipping
A-I-43	Animals	Carnivora	240	120	Silhouette chipping
A-I-44	Animals	Unidentified	200	130	Silhouette chipping
A-I-45	Animals	Unidentified	270	60	Silhouette chipping
A-I-46	Animals	Fish	560	170	Silhouette chipping
A-I-47	Animals	Fish	460	160	Silhouette chipping
A-I-48	Animals	Unidentified	380	280	Silhouette chipping
A-I-49	Animals	Unidentified	460	180	Silhouette chipping
A-I-50	Animals	Fish	650	360	Silhouette chipping
A-I-51	Animals	Unidentified	480	140	Silhouette chipping
A-I-52	Animals	Unidentified	410	160	Silhouette chipping
A-I-53	Animals	Carnivora	470	460	Silhouette chipping
A-I-54	Animals	Carnivora / Felidae	560	320	Silhouette chipping
A-I-55	Animals	Artiodactyla / Bovidae	160	80	Silhouette chipping
A-I-56	Animals	Unidentified	220	80	Silhouette chipping
A-I-57	Animals	Unidentified	420	230	Silhouette chipping
A-I-58	Animals	Unidentified	460	260	Silhouette chipping
A-I-59	Unidentified	Unidentified	130	240	Silhouette chipping
A-I-60	Animals	Artiodactyla / Cervidae	390	320	Silhouette chipping
A-I-61	Animals	Unidentified	400	120	Silhouette chipping
A-I-62	Unidentified	Unidentified	280	120	Silhouette chipping
A-I-63	Unidentified	Unidentified	510	140	Silhouette chipping

Number	Group	Type	Length (mm)	Height (mm)	Carving technique
A-I-64	Animals	Artiodactyla / Cervidae	280	220	Silhouette chipping
A-I-65	Animals	Artiodactyla / Cervidae	240	240	Silhouette chipping
A-I-66	Animals	Artiodactyla / Cervidae	340	320	Silhouette chipping
A-I-67	Animals	Unidentified	440	260	Silhouette chipping
A-I-68	Animals	Artiodactyla / Cervidae	200	200	Silhouette chipping
A-I-69	Animals	Artiodactyla / Bovidae	220	380	Silhouette chipping
A-I-70	Animals	Artiodactyla / Cervidae	1840	1570	Silhouette chipping
A-I-71	Unidentified	Unidentified	220	380	Silhouette chipping
A-I-72	Animals	Artiodactyla / Cervidae	210	280	Silhouette chipping
A-I-73	Animals	Unidentified	280	260	Silhouette chipping
A-I-74	Animals	Artiodactyla / Cervidae	220	160	Silhouette chipping
A-I-75	Animals	Unidentified	260	200	Silhouette chipping
A-I-76	Animals	Unidentified	140	150	Silhouette chipping
A-I-77	Animals	Fish	300	720	Silhouette chipping
A-I-78	Animals	Fish	140	250	Silhouette chipping
A-I-79	Animals	Unidentified	260	340	Silhouette chipping
A-I-80	Animals	Artiodactyla / Cervidae	160	240	Silhouette chipping
A-I-81	Animals	Unidentified	130	180	Silhouette chipping
A-I-82	Unidentified	Unidentified	260	240	Silhouette chipping
A-I-83	Animals	Artiodactyla / Cervidae	760	520	Silhouette chipping
A-I-84	Animals	Artiodactyla / Bovidae	600	420	Silhouette chipping
A-I-85	Animals	Artiodactyla / Cervidae	220	200	Silhouette chipping
A-I-86	Animals	Artiodactyla / Cervidae	440	400	Silhouette chipping
A-I-87	Animals	Unidentified	200	200	Silhouette chipping
A-I-88	Animals	Unidentified	300	160	Silhouette chipping
A-I-89	Unidentified	Unidentified	240	200	Silhouette chipping
A-I-90	Animals	Artiodactyla / Cervidae	220	370	Silhouette chipping
A-I-91	Animals	Artiodactyla / Unidentified	260	240	Silhouette chipping
A-I-92	Animals	Carnivora / Felidae	340	120	Silhouette chipping
A-I-93	Animals	Carnivora	400	140	Silhouette chipping
A-I-94	Animals	Artiodactyla	520	40	Silhouette chipping
A-I-95	Animals	Artiodactyla	580	260	Silhouette chipping

Number	Group	Type	Length (mm)	Height (mm)	Carving technique
A-I-96	Animals	Artiodactyla / Cervidae	240	180	Silhouette chipping
A-I-97	Animals	Snake	100	280	Silhouette chipping
A-I-98	Unidentified	Unidentified	180	220	Silhouette chipping
A-I-99	Animals	Artiodactyla	540	420	Silhouette chipping
A-I-100	Animals	Artiodactyla	240	150	Silhouette chipping
A-I-101	Unidentified	Unidentified	120	120	Silhouette chipping
A-I-102	Animals	Artiodactyla / Suideos	280	320	Silhouette chipping
A-I-103	Unidentified	Unidentified	300	320	Silhouette chipping
A-I-104	Animals	Unidentified	340	140	Silhouette chipping
A-I-105	Animals	Unidentified	340	320	Silhouette chipping
A-I-106	Animals	Artiodactyla / Bovidae	520	400	Silhouette chipping
A-I-107	Unidentified	Unidentified	760	930	Silhouette chipping
A-I-108	Animals	Unidentified	580	440	Silhouette chipping
A-I-109	Unidentified	Unidentified	350	360	Silhouette chipping
A-I-110	Unidentified	Unidentified	380	220	Silhouette chipping
A-I-111	Unidentified	Unidentified	140	80	Silhouette chipping
A-I-112	Animals	Artiodactyla / Cervidae	240	250	Silhouette chipping
A-I-113	Animals	Artiodactyla	230	180	Silhouette chipping
A-I-114	Animals	Unidentified	220	120	Silhouette chipping
A-I-115	Animals	Artiodactyla / Cervidae	340	200	Silhouette chipping
A-I-116	Unidentified	Unidentified	440	480	Silhouette chipping
A-I-117	Unidentified	Unidentified	330	480	Silhouette chipping
A-I-118	Animals	Carnivora / Felidae	560	160	Silhouette chipping
A-I-119	Animals	Artiodactyla / Cervidae	260	320	Silhouette chipping
A-I-120	Animals	Unidentified	300	200	Silhouette chipping
A-I-121	Animals	Carnivora / Felidae	580	180	Silhouette chipping
A-I-122	Unidentified	Unidentified	220	200	Silhouette chipping
A-I-123	Animals	Artiodactyla / Cervidae	160	100	Silhouette chipping
A-I-124	Animals	Carnivora / Felidae	400	100	Silhouette chipping
A-I-125	Animals	Carnivora / Felidae	460	180	Silhouette chipping
A-I-126	Animals	Artiodactyla / Suideos	300	140	Silhouette chipping
A-I-127	Animals	Artiodactyla / Bovidae	220	140	Silhouette chipping

Number	Group	Type	Length (mm)	Height (mm)	Carving technique
A-I-128	Animals	Unidentified	120	80	Silhouette chipping
A-I-129	Animals	Artiodactyla / Cervidae	280	520	Silhouette chipping
A-I-130	Animals	Unidentified	520	260	Silhouette chipping
A-I-131	Animals	Artiodactyla / Suideos	460	240	Silhouette chipping
A-I-132	Animals	Artiodactyla / Suideos	400	160	Silhouette chipping
A-I-133	Animals	Artiodactyla / Suideos	740	300	Silhouette chipping
A-I-134	Animals	Artiodactyla	500	200	Silhouette chipping
A-I-135	Animals	Unidentified	260	180	Silhouette chipping
A-I-136	Animals	Unidentified	200	140	Silhouette chipping
A-I-137	Unidentified	Unidentified	160	120	Silhouette chipping
A-I-138	Animals	Artiodactyla / Bovidae	200	280	Silhouette chipping
A-I-139	Animals	Artiodactyla / Cervidae	190	180	Silhouette chipping
A-I-140	Animals	Artiodactyla / Bovidae	180	140	Silhouette chipping
A-I-141	Animals	Artiodactyla / Cervidae	250	220	Silhouette chipping
A-I-142	Animals	Artiodactyla / Cervidae	220	240	Silhouette chipping
A-I-143	Animals	Unidentified	120	120	Silhouette chipping
A-I-144	Animals	Unidentified	160	100	Silhouette chipping
A-I-145	Animals	Artiodactyla / Cervidae	220	180	Silhouette chipping
A-I-146	Animals	Artiodactyla / Cervidae	240	240	Silhouette chipping
A-I-147	Animals	Artiodactyla / Cervidae	180	200	Silhouette chipping
A-I-148	Animals	Artiodactyla / Cervidae	160	180	Silhouette chipping
A-I-149	Humans	Full body	150	390	Silhouette chipping
A-I-150	Animals	Artiodactyla / Cervidae	140	160	Silhouette chipping
A-I-151	Plants	Flower?	120	100	Silhouette chipping
A-I-152	Animals	Artiodactyla / Cervidae	180	180	Silhouette chipping
A-I-153	Animals	Artiodactyla / Cervidae	160	140	Silhouette chipping
A-I-154	Unidentified	Unidentified	260	180	Silhouette chipping
A-I-155	Animals	Artiodactyla / Cervidae	140	160	Silhouette chipping
A-I-156	Animals	Unidentified	120	120	Silhouette chipping
A-I-157	Unidentified	Unidentified	490	960	Silhouette chipping
A-I-158	Unidentified	Unidentified	260	100	Silhouette chipping
A-I-159	Unidentified	Unidentified	100	100	Silhouette chipping

Number	Group	Type	Length (mm)	Height (mm)	Carving technique
A-I-160	Animals	Artiodactyla / Cervidae	320	160	Silhouette chipping
A-I-161	Unidentified	Unidentified	420	180	Silhouette chipping
A-I-162	Unidentified	Unidentified	24	280	Silhouette chipping
A-I-163	Animals	Artiodactyla / Cervidae	600	520	Silhouette chipping
A-I-164	Animals	Artiodactyla / Cervidae	360	440	Silhouette chipping
A-I-165	Animals	Artiodactyla / Cervidae	240	360	Silhouette chipping
A-I-166-1	Animals	Artiodactyla / Suideos	732	260	Silhouette chipping
A-I-166-2	Animals	Artiodactyla / Suideos	388	284	Silhouette chipping
A-I-167	Unidentified	Unidentified	460	380	Silhouette chipping
A-I-168	Animals	Artiodactyla	240	280	Silhouette chipping
A-I-169	Unidentified	Unidentified	980	1140	Silhouette chipping
A-I-170	Animals	Unidentified	150	80	Silhouette chipping
A-I-171	Animals	Unidentified	270	220	Silhouette chipping
A-I-172	Animals	Unidentified	220	240	Silhouette chipping
A-I-173	Animals	Carnivora / Felidae	180	60	Silhouette chipping
A-I-174	Animals	Carnivora / Felidae	280	220	Silhouette chipping
A-I-175	Animals	Carnivora	250	190	Silhouette chipping
A-I-176	Animals	Artiodactyla / Cervidae	280	220	Silhouette chipping
A-I-177	Unidentified	Unidentified	740	380	Silhouette chipping
A-I-178	Animals	Unidentified	300	140	Silhouette chipping
A-I-179	Animals	Unidentified	230	100	Silhouette chipping
A-I-180	Animals	Carnivora / Felidae	220	180	Silhouette chipping
A-I-181	Animals	Carnivora / Felidae	200	140	Silhouette chipping
A-I-182	Animals	Felidae	200	100	Silhouette chipping
A-I-183	Animals	Artiodactyla	180	140	Silhouette chipping
A-I-184	Animals	Artiodactyla / Cervidae	740	580	Silhouette chipping
A-I-185	Animals	Unidentified	1340	820	Silhouette chipping
A-I-186	Animals	Unidentified	200	220	Silhouette chipping
A-I-187	Animals	Unidentified	260	440	Silhouette chipping
A-I-188	Animals	Artiodactyla / Cervidae	300	180	Silhouette chipping
A-I-189	Animals	Unidentified	500	180	Silhouette chipping
A-I-190	Animals	Carnivora / Felidae	520	220	Silhouette chipping

Number	Group	Type	Length (mm)	Height (mm)	Carving technique
A-I-191	Animals	Artiodactyla / Cervidae	220	140	Silhouette chipping
A-I-192	Animals	Carnivora / Felidae	55	360	Silhouette chipping
A-I-193	Unidentified	Unidentified	220	180	Silhouette chipping
A-I-194	Animals	Artiodactyla / Cervidae	260	200	Silhouette chipping
A-I-195	Animals	Carnivora	240	120	Silhouette chipping
A-I-196	Animals	Unidentified	210	120	Silhouette chipping
A-I-197	Animals	Unidentified	330	220	Silhouette chipping
A-I-198	Animals	Unidentified	240	220	Silhouette chipping
A-I-199	Animals	Unidentified	270	200	Silhouette chipping
A-I-200	Animals	Artiodactyla / Suideos	620	240	Silhouette chipping
A-I-201	Animals	Unidentified	340	140	Silhouette chipping
A-I-202	Animals	Artiodactyla / Suideos	620	240	Silhouette chipping
A-I-203	Animals	Carnivora / Felidae	340	240	Silhouette chipping
A-I-204	Animals	Artiodactyla / Cervidae	1300	980	Silhouette chipping
A-I-205	Animals	Unidentified	260	140	Silhouette chipping
A-I-206	Animals	Unidentified	530	320	Silhouette chipping
A-I-207	Animals	Artiodactyla / Cervidae	560	720	Silhouette chipping
A-I-208	Animals	Artiodactyla / Cervidae	200	440	Silhouette chipping
A-I-209	Animals	Artiodactyla / Cervidae	140	240	Silhouette chipping
A-I-210	Animals	Carnivora / Felidae	240	120	Silhouette chipping
A-I-211	Animals	Unidentified	210	180	Silhouette chipping
A-I-212	Animals	Artiodactyla / Bovidae	430	140	Silhouette chipping
A-I-213	Unidentified	Unidentified	200	300	Silhouette chipping
A-I-214-1	Animals	Unidentified	120	60	Silhouette chipping
A-I-214-2	Animals	Artiodactyla / Cervidae	160	80	Silhouette chipping
Total	217 engravings				

1) Animals

There are 216 animal figures on Panel A, 180 of them depicted in silhouette by chipping (A-1), and 35 detailed drawings engraved with fine lines (A-TLE). Among the animals in A-I, deer and artiodactyls account for 56% (121), carnivores 12% (26), fish 3% (6), and unidentified creatures 27% (57). Among the figures of A-I, a number of animals are represented in pairs (1-2, 9-10, 12-13, 21-22, 23-24, 175-176). On the other hand, the deer around the human figure (A-I-149) are grouped together (A-I-146, 148, 152). A-I-166-1 and 166-2 appear to be a type of boar. One of them is depicted on top of the other, suggesting mating. Many other animals overlap with each other, entirely or partly. A-I-77 and 78 are fish, but considering the proximity of the nearby Bangudae, there is a good possibility that these figures are whales. The majority of figures engraved with thin lines are horses (27 figures). These horses (A-TLE-73 and 99, for example) are depicted with only characteristic features. There are also two birds (A-TLE-69) and four dragons (A-TLE-42, 72, 115, 119).

Fig. 7. A-I, individual figures 1 (1~68)

Fig. 8. A-I, individual figures 2 (69~114)

Fig. 9. A-I, individual figures 3 (115~179)

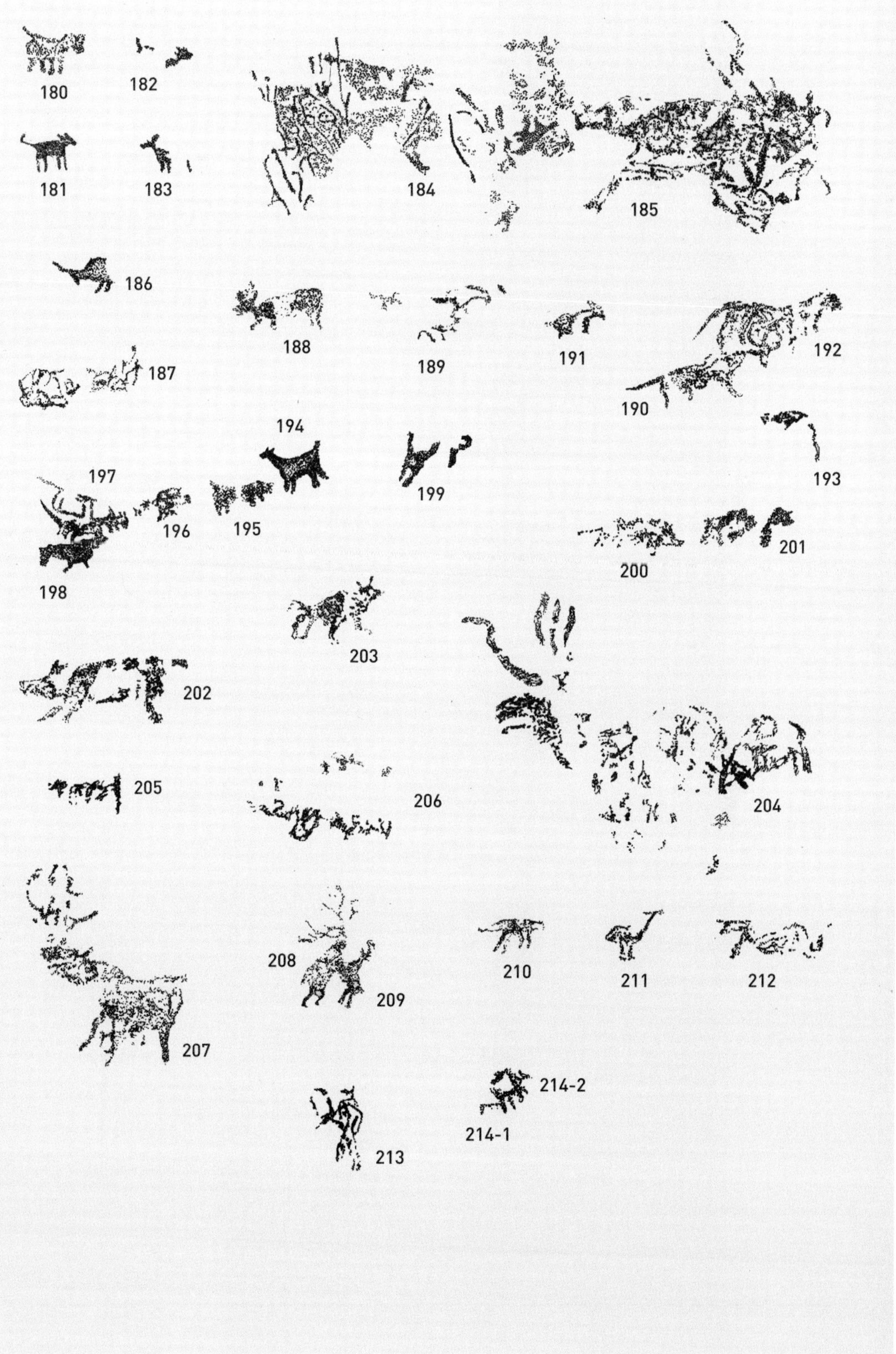

Fig. 10. A-I, individual figures 4 (180~213)

Table 4. Classification of individual figures (A-II)

Number	Group	Type	Length (mm)	Height (mm)	Carving technique
A-II-1	Unidentified	Unidentified	450	580	Outline chipping
A-II-2	Geometric patterns	Lozenges / Horizontal	220	320	Outline chipping
A-II-3	Geometric patterns	Unidentified	300	220	Outline chipping
A-II-4	Geometric patterns	Lozenges / Vertical	300	760	Outline chipping
A-II-5	Geometric patterns	Lozenges / Vertical	380	1360	Outline chipping
A-II-6	Geometric patterns	Lozenges / Vertical	320	700	Outline chipping
A-II-7	Geometric patterns	Unidentified	220	280	Outline chipping
A-II-8	Geometric patterns	Lozenges / Vertical	360	840	Outline chipping
A-II-9	Geometric patterns	Waves	600	500	Outline chipping
A-II-10	Geometric patterns	Circles / Divided	160	160	Outline chipping
A-II-11	Geometric patterns	Lozenges / Vertical	380	440	Outline chipping
A-II-12	Geometric patterns	Lozenges / Vertical	440	220	Outline chipping
A-II-13	Geometric patterns	Lozenges / Vertical	380	540	Outline chipping
A-II-14-1	Geometric patterns	Lozenges / Horizontal&Vertical	700	940	Outline chipping
A-II-14-2	Humans?	Unidentified	250	560	Outline chipping
A-II-15	Geometric patterns	Circles / Divided	340	1240	Outline chipping
A-II-16	Geometric patterns	Lozenges / Vertical	320	720	Outline chipping
A-II-17	Geometric patterns	Lozenges / Horizontal	520	300	Outline chipping
A-II-18	Unidentified	Unidentified	1100	840	Outline chipping
A-II-19	Unidentified	Unidentified	440	640	Outline chipping
A-II-20	Geometric patterns	Circles / Single	120	140	Outline chipping
A-II-21	Geometric patterns	Circles / Single	160	100	Outline chipping
A-II-22	Geometric patterns	Circles / Single	140	200	Outline chipping
A-II-23	Geometric patterns	Circles / Circle with a tale	180	200	Outline chipping
A-II-24	Geometric patterns	Lozenges / Horizontal&Vertical	600	820	Outline chipping
A-II-25	Geometric patterns	Circles / Concentric circles	260	220	Outline chipping
A-II-26	Geometric patterns	Waves / Vertical	200	1330	Outline chipping
A-II-27	Geometric patterns	Waves / Vertical	124	230	Outline chipping
A-II-28	Geometric patterns	Unidentified	270	240	Outline chipping
A-II-29	Geometric patterns	Lozenges / Vertical	30	200	Outline chipping
A-II-30	Geometric patterns	Lozenges / Horizontal	1580	440	Outline chipping
A-II-31	Geometric patterns	Circles / Circle with a tale	280	410	Outline chipping

Number	Group	Type	Length (mm)	Height (mm)	Carving technique
A-II-32	Geometric patterns	Lozenges / Horizontal&Vertical	540	760	Outline chipping
A-II-33	Humans	Full body	300	440	Outline chipping
A-II-34	Geometric patterns	Lozenges / Horizontal&Vertical	370	330	Outline chipping
A-II-35	Geometric patterns	Circles / Concentric circles	220	240	Outline chipping
A-II-36	Geometric patterns	Circles / Single	170	240	Outline chipping
A-II-37	Humans	Full body	220	620	Outline chipping
A-II-38	Geometric patterns	Lozenges	100	320	Outline chipping
A-II-39	Unidentified	Unidentified	960	860	Outline chipping
A-II-40	Unidentified	Unidentified	270	260	Outline chipping
A-II-41	Geometric patterns	Lozenges / Horizontal&Vertical	320	580	Outline chipping
A-II-42	Geometric patterns	Lozenges / Horizontal&Vertical	390	640	Outline chipping
A-II-43	Geometric patterns	Circles / Concentric circles	420	420	Outline chipping
A-II-44	Geometric patterns	Circles / Concentric circles	190	240	Outline chipping
A-II-45	Geometric patterns	Circles / Linked circle	640	480	Outline chipping
A-II-46	Humans	Face	460	500	Outline chipping
A-II-47	Geometric patterns	Unidentified	800	580	Outline chipping
A-II-48	Unidentified	Unidentified	740	780	Outline chipping
A-II-49	Geometric patterns	Lozenges / Horizontal	500	440	Outline chipping
A-II-50	Geometric patterns	Lozenges / Horizontal&Vertical	480	480	Outline chipping
A-II-51	Geometric patterns	Circles / Single	140	120	Outline chipping
A-II-52	Geometric patterns	Lozenges / Vertical	520	800	Outline chipping
A-II-53	Geometric patterns	Lozenges / Horizontal&Vertical	700	560	Outline chipping
A-II-54	Unidentified	Unidentified	360	320	Outline chipping
A-II-55	Geometric patterns	Lozenges / Divided	280	360	Outline chipping
A-II-56	Geometric patterns	Lozenges / Single	220	260	Outline chipping
A-II-57	Humans	Full body	280	490	Outline chipping
A-II-58	Unidentified	Unidentified	340	600	Outline chipping
A-II-59	Geometric patterns	Circles / Divided	320	400	Outline chipping
A-II-60	Geometric patterns	Waves	600	520	Outline chipping
A-II-61	Unidentified	Unidentified	960	860	Outline chipping
A-II-62	Unidentified	Unidentified	430	720	Outline chipping
A-II-63	Geometric patterns	Waves	250	440	Outline chipping

Number	Group	Type	Length (mm)	Height (mm)	Carving technique
A-II-64	Geometric patterns	Lozenges / Single	250	200	Outline chipping
A-II-65	Humans	Full body	430	720	Outline chipping
A-II-66	Geometric patterns	Circles / Single	200	460	Outline chipping
A-II-67	Geometric patterns	Circles / Single	200	380	Outline chipping
A-II-68	Humans?	Full body	320	520	Outline chipping
A-II-69	Humans?	Full body	440	540	Outline chipping
A-II-70	Geometric patterns	Waves	420	260	Outline chipping
A-II-71	Unidentified	Unidentified	350	320	Outline chipping
A-II-72	Humans	Full body	200	920	Outline chipping
A-II-73	Unidentified	Unidentified	200	300	Outline chipping
A-II-74	Unidentified	Unidentified	300	240	Outline chipping
A-II-75	Humans?	Full body	340	560	Outline chipping
A-II-76	Unidentified	Unidentified	700	620	Outline chipping
A-II-77	Geometric patterns	Lozenges / Single	140	180	Outline chipping
A-II-78	Geometric patterns	Lozenges / Single	640	300	Outline chipping
A-II-79	Geometric patterns	Circles / Concentric circles	280	270	Outline chipping
A-II-80	Geometric patterns	Circles / Concentric circles	140	130	Outline chipping
A-II-81	Geometric patterns	Waves	560	450	Outline chipping
A-II-82	Geometric patterns	Lozenges / Vertical	110	110	Outline chipping
A-II-83	Unidentified	Unidentified	290	180	Outline chipping
A-II-84	Geometric patterns	Waves	420	360	Outline chipping
A-II-85	Geometric patterns	Circles / Single	90	80	Outline chipping
A-II-86	Geometric patterns	Circles / Circle with a tale	100	140	Outline chipping
A-II-87	Unidentified	Unidentified	240	220	Outline chipping
A-II-88	Unidentified	Unidentified	240	180	Outline chipping
A-II-89	Geometric patterns	Circles / Concentric circles	300	280	Outline chipping
A-II-90	Unidentified	Unidentified	360	650	Outline chipping
A-II-91	Unidentified	Unidentified	770	560	Outline chipping
A-II-92	Unidentified	Unidentified	510	480	Outline chipping
A-II-93	Geometric patterns	Circles / Circle with a tale	264	200	Outline chipping
A-II-94	Geometric patterns	Lozenges / Horizontal	300	180	Outline chipping
A-II-95	Unidentified	Unidentified	80	100	Outline chipping

Number	Group	Type	Length (mm)	Height (mm)	Carving technique
A-II-96	Unidentified	Unidentified	840	280	Outline chipping
A-II-97	Unidentified	Unidentified	900	220	Outline chipping
A-II-98	Geometric patterns	Circles / Divided	760	140	Outline chipping
A-II-99	Geometric patterns	Waves	140	90	Outline chipping
A-II-100	Unidentified	Unidentified	680	120	Outline chipping
A-II-101	Animals	Artiodactyla / Unidentified	280	300	Outline chipping
A-II-102	Geometric patterns	Lozenges / Single	210	280	Outline chipping
A-II-103	Geometric patterns	Lozenges	140	400	Outline chipping
A-II-104	Geometric patterns	Lozenges / Vertical	180	290	Outline chipping
A-II-105	Geometric patterns	Circles / Circle with a tale	380	220	Outline chipping
A-II-106	Unidentified	Unidentified	400	250	Outline chipping
A-II-107	Geometric patterns	Circles / Linked circle	370	160	Outline chipping
A-II-108	Geometric patterns	Lozenges / Single	260	340	Outline chipping
A-II-109	Geometric patterns	Circles / Circle with a tale	120	160	Outline chipping
A-II-110	Unidentified	Unidentified	80	200	Outline chipping
A-II-111	Unidentified	Unidentified	130	530	Outline chipping
A-II-112	Geometric patterns	Circles / Circle with a tale	180	210	Outline chipping
A-II-113	Geometric patterns	Lozenges / Horizontal&Vertical	780	680	Outline chipping
A-II-114	Unidentified	Unidentified	120	280	Outline chipping
A-II-115	Geometric patterns	Lozenges / Single	210	180	Outline chipping
A-II-116	Unidentified	Unidentified	400	460	Outline chipping
A-II-117	Unidentified	Unidentified	640	300	Outline chipping
A-II-118	Geometric patterns	Lozenges / Single	260	320	Outline chipping
A-II-119	Unidentified	Unidentified	280	400	Outline chipping
A-II-120	Unidentified	Unidentified	500	640	Outline chipping
A-II-121	Geometric patterns	Lozenges	120	220	Outline chipping
A-II-122	Geometric patterns	Lozenges	170	80	Outline chipping
A-II-123	Unidentified	Unidentified	700	980	Outline chipping
A-II-124	Unidentified	Unidentified	110	190	Outline chipping
A-II-125	Unidentified	Unidentified	120	160	Outline chipping
A-II-126	Unidentified	Unidentified	840	870	Outline chipping
A-II-127	Geometric patterns	Lozenges / Horizontal&Vertical	520	580	Outline chipping

Number	Group	Type	Length (mm)	Height (mm)	Carving technique
A-II-128	Unidentified	Unidentified	260	980	Outline chipping
A-II-129	Geometric patterns	Circles / Divided	150	580	Outline chipping
A-II-130	Geometric patterns	Lozenges / Vertical	520	410	Outline chipping
A-II-131	Geometric patterns	Waves	500	340	Outline chipping
A-II-132	Unidentified	Unidentified	360	310	Outline chipping
A-II-133	Unidentified	Unidentified	600	240	Outline chipping
A-II-134	Geometric patterns	Lozenges / Single	80	80	Outline chipping
Total	135 engravings				

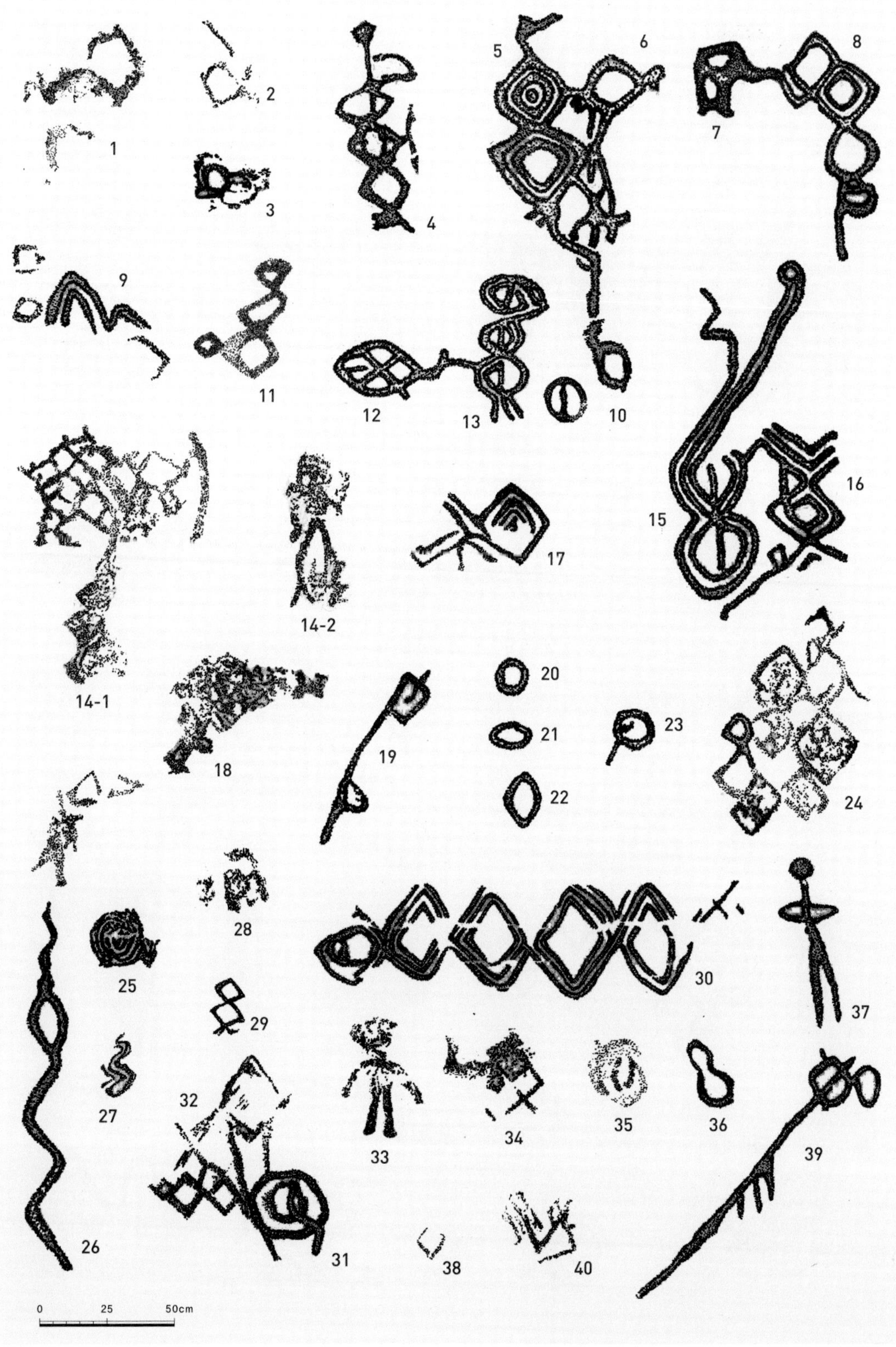

Fig. 11. A-II, individual figures 1 (1~40)

Fig. 12. A-II, individual figures 2 (41~84)

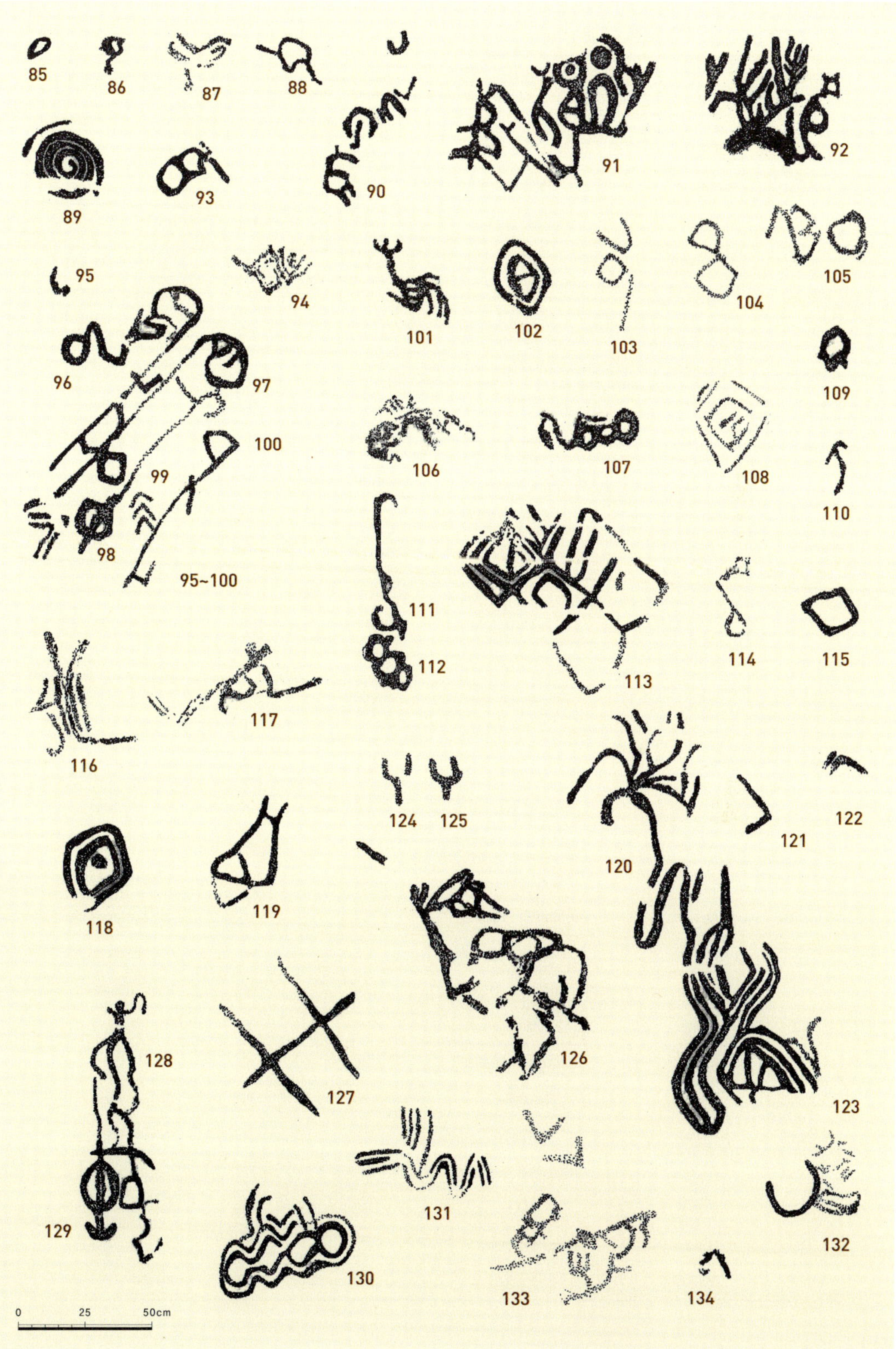

Fig. 13. A-II, individual figures 3 (85~134)

Table 5. Classification of individual figures (A-TLE)

Number	Group	Type	Length (mm)	Height (mm)	Carving technique
A-TLE-1	Plants	Tree	540	720	Thin-line engraving
A-TLE-2	Humans	Full body	200	620	Thin-line engraving
A-TLE-3	Humans	Full body	180	380	Thin-line engraving
A-TLE-4	Animals	Artiodactyla / Equidae	340	160	Thin-line engraving
A-TLE-5-1	Animals	Artiodactyla / Equidae	540	510	Thin-line engraving
A-TLE-5-2	Animals	Artiodactyla / Cervidae	124	420	Thin-line engraving
A-TLE-5-3	Animals	Artiodactyla / Cervidae	280	440	Thin-line engraving
A-TLE-6	Humans	Mounted figures	170	140	Thin-line engraving
A-TLE-7-1	Humans	Mounted figures	358	188	Thin-line engraving
A-TLE-7-2	Animals	Artiodactyla / Equidae	144	90	Thin-line engraving
A-TLE-8	Animals	Artiodactyla / Equidae	360	180	Thin-line engraving
A-TLE-9	Animals	Artiodactyla / Equidae	260	190	Thin-line engraving
A-TLE-10	Plants	Thunder?	250	720	Thin-line engraving
A-TLE-11	Tools	Net	480	880	Thin-line engraving
A-TLE-12	Humans	Full body	160	500	Thin-line engraving
A-TLE-13	Humans	Mounted figures	500	260	Thin-line engraving
A-TLE-14	Humans	Mounted figures	160	190	Thin-line engraving
A-TLE-15	Animals	Artiodactyla / Equidae	20	20	Thin-line engraving
A-TLE-16	Animals	Artiodactyla / Equidae	80	40	Thin-line engraving
A-TLE-17	Humans	Mounted figures	120	60	Thin-line engraving
A-TLE-18	Animals	Artiodactyla / Equidae	200	80	Thin-line engraving
A-TLE-19-1	Humans	Mounted figures	232	156	Thin-line engraving
A-TLE-19-2	Animals	Artiodactyla / Equidae	154	40	Thin-line engraving
A-TLE-20	Animals	Artiodactyla / Equidae	120	60	Thin-line engraving
A-TLE-21-1	Plants	Forest? / Complex composition	1240	1560	Thin-line engraving
A-TLE-21-2	Humans	Mounted figures	270	300	Thin-line engraving
A-TLE-22	Animals	Artiodactyla / Equidae	340	360	Thin-line engraving
A-TLE-23	Tools	Umbrella	340	360	Thin-line engraving
A-TLE-24	Humans	Full body	300	340	Thin-line engraving
A-TLE-25	Animals	Artiodactyla / Equidae	340	220	Thin-line engraving
A-TLE-26	Plants?	Tree?	160	1100	Thin-line engraving
A-TLE-27	Humans	Mounted figures	400	300	Thin-line engraving
A-TLE-28	Animals?	Unidentified	120	70	Thin-line engraving

Number	Group	Type	Length (mm)	Height (mm)	Carving technique
A-TLE-29	Man-made structures	Ship	1400	1060	Thin-line engraving
A-TLE-30	Man-made structures	Watch tower?	260	600	Thin-line engraving
A-TLE-31	Man-made structures?	Port?	1440	1500	Thin-line engraving
A-TLE-32	Unidentified	Unidentified	320	450	Thin-line engraving
A-TLE-33	Humans	Full body	160	340	Thin-line engraving
A-TLE-34	Humans	Full body	200	230	Thin-line engraving
A-TLE-35	Humans	Mounted figures	390	240	Thin-line engraving
A-TLE-36	Animals	Artiodactyla / Equidae	340	110	Thin-line engraving
A-TLE-37	Humans	Full body	130	220	Thin-line engraving
A-TLE-38	Plants?	Unidentified	100	220	Thin-line engraving
A-TLE-39	Man-made structures	Ship?	460	480	Thin-line engraving
A-TLE-40	Man-made structures	Ship	520	440	Thin-line engraving
A-TLE-41	Man-made structures	Ship?	440	220	Thin-line engraving
A-TLE-42	Animals	Dragon	1440	770	Thin-line engraving
A-TLE-43	Plants	Tree?	200	220	Thin-line engraving
A-TLE-44	Humans	Mounted figures	360	400	Thin-line engraving
A-TLE-45	Humans	Full body	240	300	Thin-line engraving
A-TLE-46	Humans	Full body	300	280	Thin-line engraving
A-TLE-47	Unidentified	Unidentified	560	300	Thin-line engraving
A-TLE-48	Animals	Artiodactyla / Equidae	250	160	Thin-line engraving
A-TLE-49	Humans	Mounted figures	520	440	Thin-line engraving
A-TLE-50	Humans	Mounted figures	120	120	Thin-line engraving
A-TLE-51	Humans	Mounted figures	240	180	Thin-line engraving
A-TLE-52	Humans	Mounted figures	180	110	Thin-line engraving
A-TLE-53	Animals	Artiodactyla / Equidae	420	120	Thin-line engraving
A-TLE-54	Humans	Mounted figures	330	200	Thin-line engraving
A-TLE-55	Humans	Mounted figures	200	140	Thin-line engraving
A-TLE-56	Unidentified	Unidentified	240	220	Thin-line engraving
A-TLE-57	Unidentified	Unidentified	230	360	Thin-line engraving
A-TLE-58	Plants?	Tree?	140	200	Thin-line engraving
A-TLE-59	Unidentified	Unidentified	270	220	Thin-line engraving
A-TLE-60	Unidentified	Unidentified	440	300	Thin-line engraving
A-TLE-61	Unidentified	Unidentified	200	160	Thin-line engraving

Number	Group	Type	Length (mm)	Height (mm)	Carving technique
A-TLE-62	Humans	Full body	120	120	Thin-line engraving
A-TLE-63	Humans	Mounted figures	290	120	Thin-line engraving
A-TLE-64	Humans / Complex composition	Full body	390	480	Thin-line engraving
A-TLE-65	Humans	Full body	240	180	Thin-line engraving
A-TLE-66	Humans	Mounted figures	180	120	Thin-line engraving
A-TLE-67	Humans	Mounted figures	140	120	Thin-line engraving
A-TLE-68	Unidentified	Unidentified	130	160	Thin-line engraving
A-TLE-69	Animals	Bird	260	480	Thin-line engraving
A-TLE-70	Plants?	Tree?	440	410	Thin-line engraving
A-TLE-71	Humans	Full body	300	420	Thin-line engraving
A-TLE-72	Animals	Dragon?	540	100	Thin-line engraving
A-TLE-73-1	Animals	Artiodactyla / Equidae	380	150	Thin-line engraving
A-TLE-73-2	Man-made structures	Watch tower?	180	530	Thin-line engraving
A-TLE-74	Humans	Lower body	360	460	Thin-line engraving
A-TLE-75	Plants	Forest?	1960	2480	Thin-line engraving
A-TLE-76-1	Animals	Artiodactyla / Equidae	780	350	Thin-line engraving
A-TLE-76-2	Unidentified	Unidentified	110	260	Thin-line engraving
A-TLE-76-3	Man-made structures	House, Ship?	420	280	Thin-line engraving
A-TLE-77	Unidentified	Egg?	180	320	Silhouette chipping
A-TLE-78	Humans	Box and figure?	240	240	Thin-line engraving
A-TLE-79	Unidentified	Light?	1800	1180	Thin-line engraving
A-TLE-80	Animals	Artiodactyla / Equidae	260	180	Thin-line engraving
A-TLE-81	Animals	Artiodactyla / Equidae	360	240	Thin-line engraving
A-TLE-82	Man-made structures	Ship?	740	670	Thin-line engraving
A-TLE-83	Humans	Mounted figures	280	140	Thin-line engraving
A-TLE-84	Animals	Unidentified	160	60	Thin-line engraving
A-TLE-85	Humans	Mounted figures	190	220	Thin-line engraving
A-TLE-86	Humans	Mounted figures	200	260	Thin-line engraving
A-TLE-87	Animals	Bird?	260	340	Thin-line engraving
A-TLE-88	Humans	Full body	120	320	Thin-line engraving
A-TLE-89	Man-made structures	Ship	560	540	Thin-line engraving
A-TLE-90	Man-made structures	Ship	760	890	Thin-line engraving

Number	Group	Type	Length (mm)	Height (mm)	Carving technique
A-TLE-91	Man-made structures	Ship	840	80	Thin-line engraving
A-TLE-92	Man-made structures	Ship	640	200	Thin-line engraving
A-TLE-93	Humans	Full body	490	220	Thin-line engraving
A-TLE-94	Animals	Artiodactyla / Equidae	400	320	Thin-line engraving
A-TLE-95	Plants	Group of trees	340	1270	Thin-line engraving
A-TLE-96	Plants	Tree	760	1760	Thin-line engraving
A-TLE-97	Plants	Tree	220	960	Thin-line engraving
A-TLE-98	Plants	Tree	120	460	Thin-line engraving
A-TLE-99	Animals	Artiodactyla / Equidae	180	460	Thin-line engraving
A-TLE-100	Animals	Artiodactyla / Equidae	60	80	Thin-line engraving
A-TLE-101	Animals	Artiodactyla / Suideos	80	60	Thin-line engraving
A-TLE-102	Man-made structures	Ship?	500	540	Thin-line engraving
A-TLE-103	Animals	Artiodactyla / Equidae	80	60	Thin-line engraving
A-TLE-104	Humans	Full body	140	380	Thin-line engraving
A-TLE-105	Plants	Tree	480	930	Thin-line engraving
A-TLE-106	Humans	Full body	140	530	Thin-line engraving
A-TLE-107	Animals	Artiodactyla / Equidae	80	40	Thin-line engraving
A-TLE-108	Man-made structures	Watch tower?	40	80	Thin-line engraving
A-TLE-109	Unidentified	Unidentified	150	220	Thin-line engraving
A-TLE-110	Humans	Mounted figures	140	170	Thin-line engraving
A-TLE-111	Man-made structures	Tower	600	1160	Thin-line engraving
A-TLE-112	Man-made structures	Watch tower?	220	1020	Thin-line engraving
A-TLE-113	Unidentified	Unidentified	1860	1140	Thin-line engraving
A-TLE-114	Humans	Full body	400	1000	Thin-line engraving
A-TLE-115	Animals	Dragon	1090	460	Thin-line engraving
A-TLE-116	Man-made structures	Watch tower?	190	620	Thin-line engraving
A-TLE-117	Humans	Full body	160	420	Thin-line engraving
A-TLE-118	Humans	Full body	150	300	Thin-line engraving
A-TLE-119	Animals	Dragon?	280	520	Thin-line engraving
Total	127 engravings				

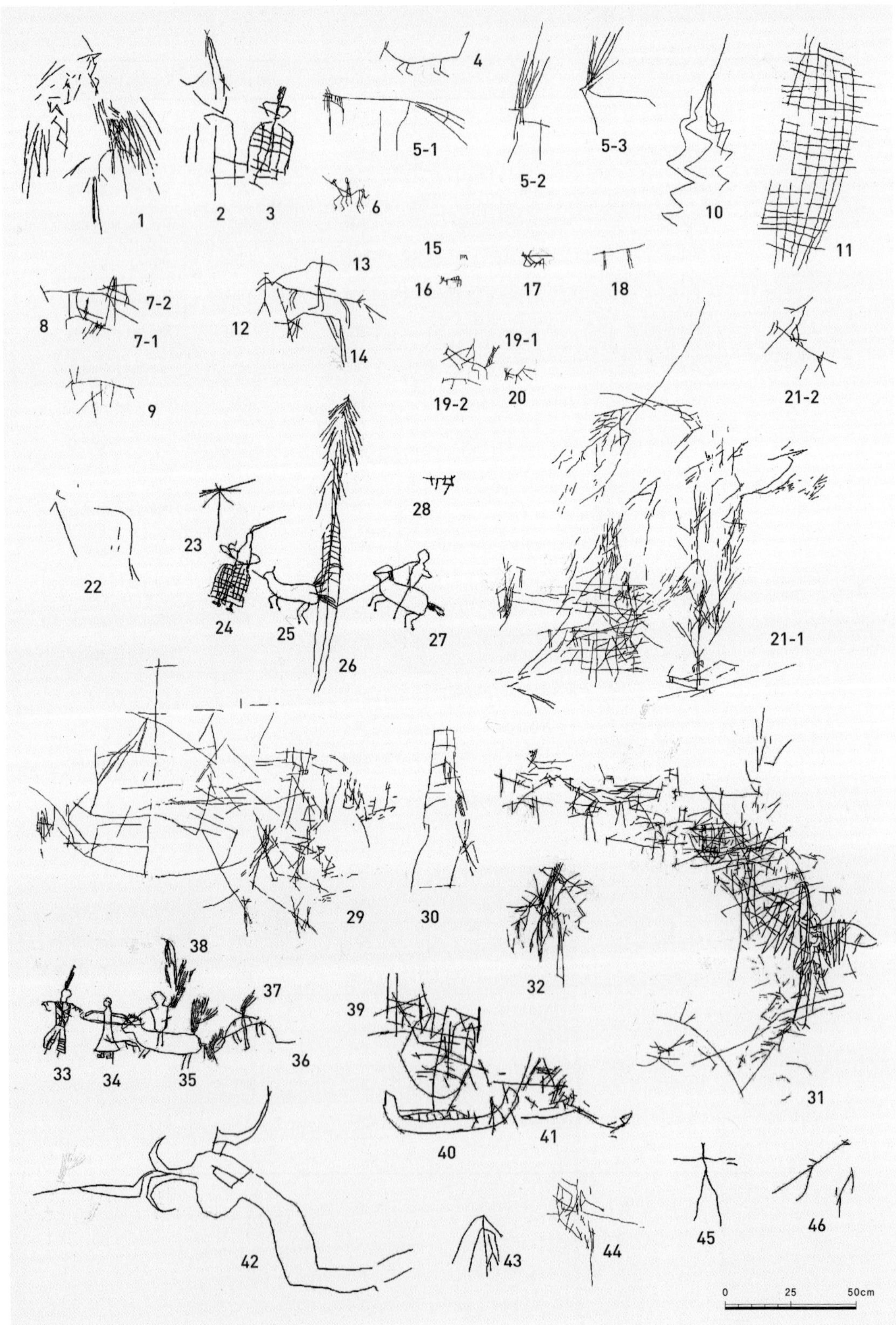

Fig. 14. A-TLE, individual figures 1 (1~46)

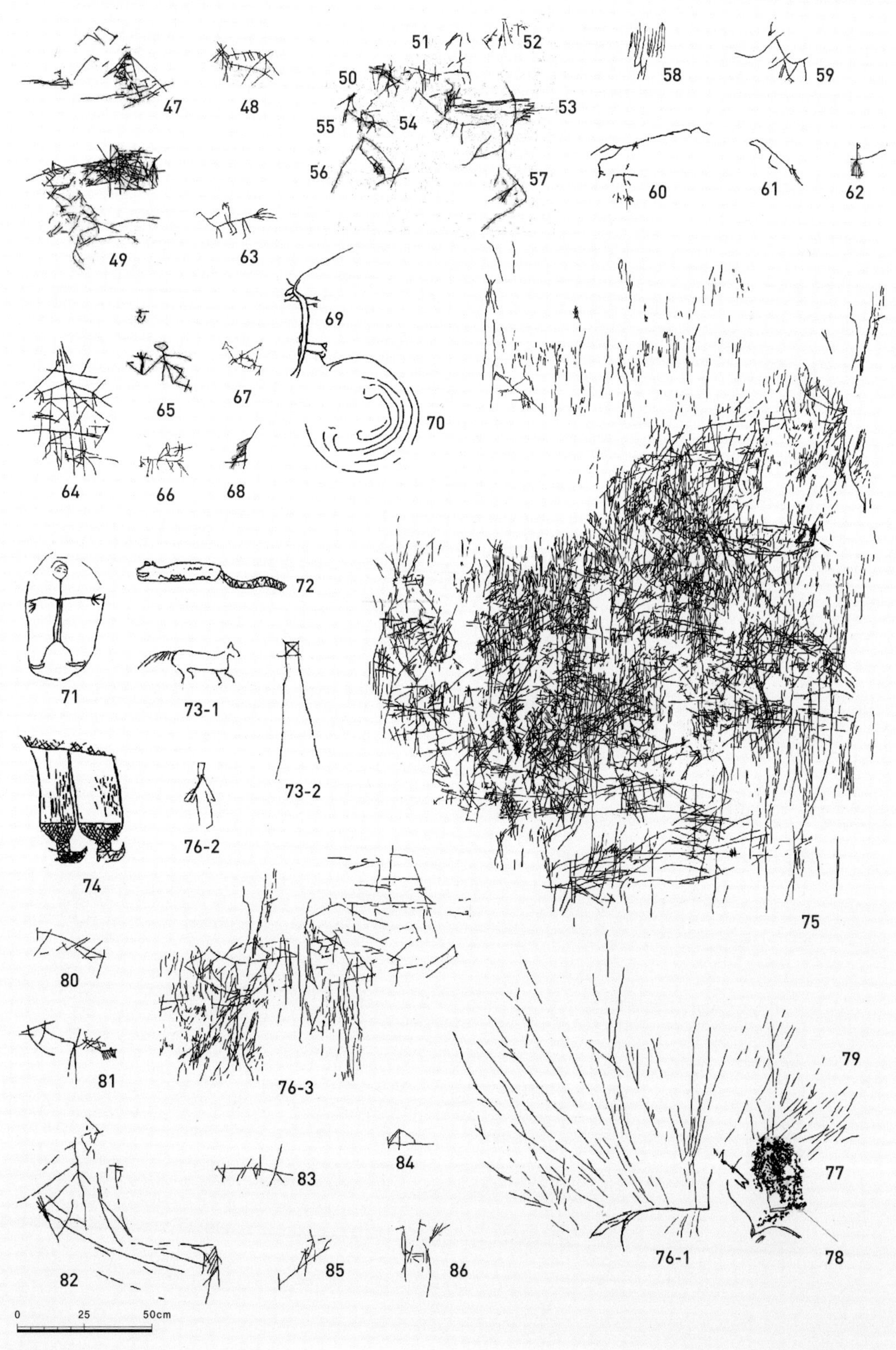

Fig. 15. A-TLE, individual figures 2 (47~86)

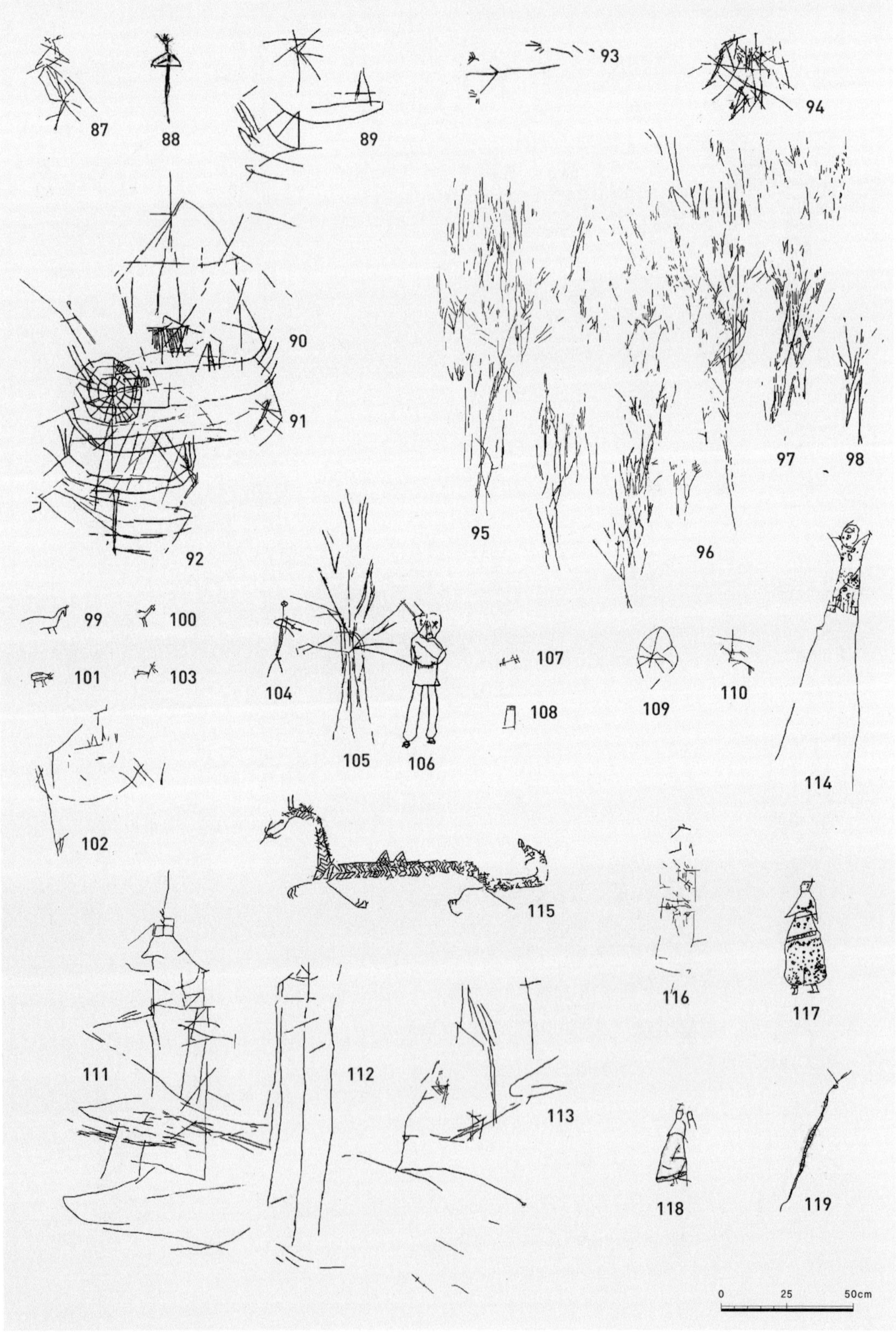

Fig. 16. A-TLE, individual figures 3 (87~119)

Photo 7. Panel A, animals (A-I-12, 13)

Photo 8. Panel A, animals (A-I-21, 22)

Photo 9. Panel A, animals (A-I-23, 24)

2) Human Figures

There are 59 human figures on Panel A, including four silhouette figures on A-I and ten on A-II, the "geometric section." The one holding a bow (A-I-14) and the other full body figure (A-I-149) are located near animals. Some figures take the "mask" form with animal bodies, which have been particularly noted since the discovery of the Cheonjeon-ri Petroglyphs. Human figures represented as simplified symbols (A-II-37, 46, 57, 72) are also very characteristic. There are 45 human figures on section A-TLE. Most of them are in procession scenes depicted on the lower part of the panel and many of them are riding or leading horses. Not far from the left end of the panel is a man wearing checkered pants heading to the left. At some distance from this man is a procession scene also heading toward the left side of the rock. The procession is led by a man in checkered pants leading a horse, followed by a person in striped pants, another person wearing a skirt, and a number of mounted figures. Two sail boats follow this procession (Jeon 1999). On the lower right part of the panel is a dragon with a long, slender body (A-TLE-115) and other human figures (A-TLE-114, 117, 118).

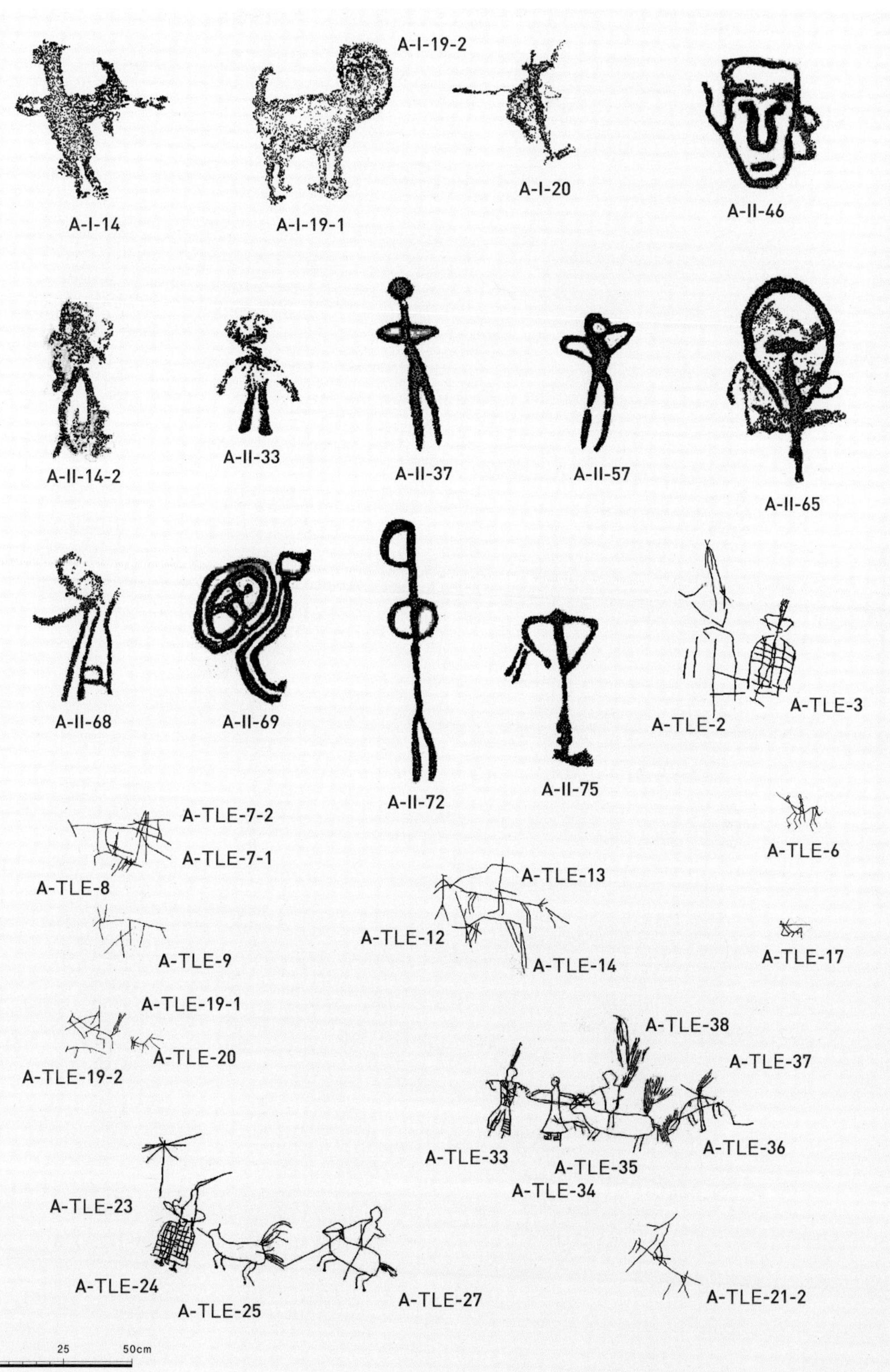

Fig. 17. Panel A, humans 1

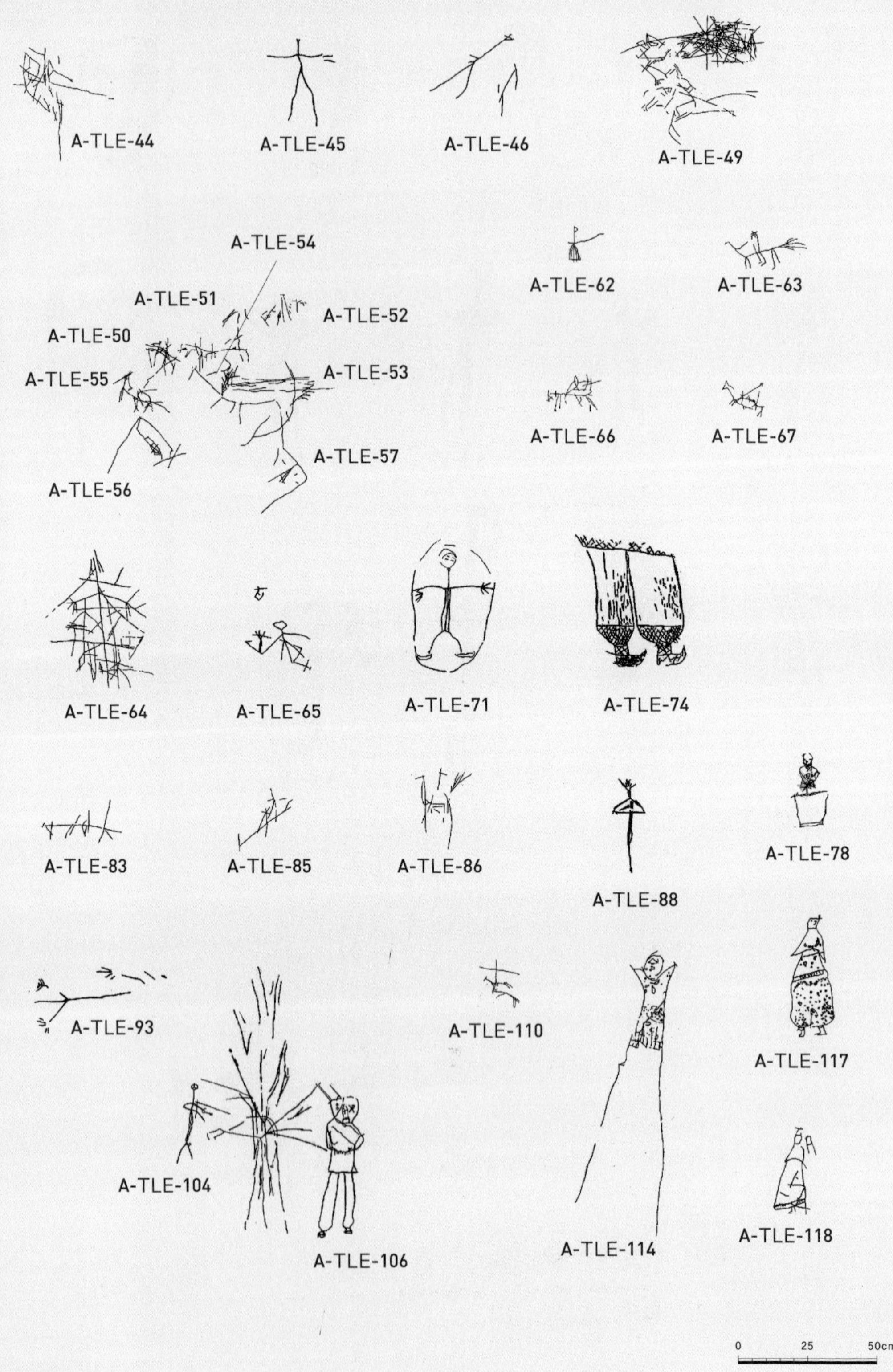

Fig. 18. Panel A, humans 2

Photo 10. Panel A, humans (A-I-14)

Photo 11. Panel A, humans (A-I-19-1, 19-2)

3) Geometric Patterns

There are 86 geometric patterns on A-II. Most of them are linked to each other so separating them into individual figures is not easy. The patterns, mostly lozenges, circles, and waves, are linked vertically and horizontally in pairs or in groups. Some of them are double or triple-engraved. Many lozenges are double-lined and divided vertically. Some have x marks inside and a squiggle, a shape that resembles a fish. The double circles (A-II-43) and lozenges (A-II-5, 52) located on the middle and upper part of this section are engraved very deeply, which makes them more distinctive when compared to the other figures. On the other hand, the geometric patterns located on the right walls are not only in bad condition but look unfinished. There are 42 lozenges, 29 circles, 10 waves, and 5 unidentifiable geometrics patterns on Panel A. One Lozenges, one circle, and two waves are visible on Panel D, and there are some traces of geometric patterns on Panel C.

Photo 12. Panel A, geometric patterns (A-II-5, 6)

Photo 13. Panel A, geometric patterns (A-II-12, 13)

Photo 14. Panel A, geometric patterns (A-II-15~17)

Photo 15. Panel A, geometric patterns (A-II-26)

Photo 16. Panel A, geometric patterns (A-II-30~50)

Photo 17. Panel A, geometric patterns (A-II-42~58)

Photo 18. Panel A, geometric patterns (A-II-55~60)

Photo 19. Panel A, geometric patterns (A-II-89~92)

Photo 20. Panel A, geometric patterns (A-II-118~123)

Photo 21. Panel A, geometric patterns (A-II-129)

Photo 22. Panel A, thin-line engravings (A-TLE-24~27)

Photo 23. Panel A, thin-line engravings (A-TLE-35~37)

Photo 24. Panel A, thin-line engravings (A-TLE-69)

Photo 25. Panel A, thin-line engravings (A-TLE-71)

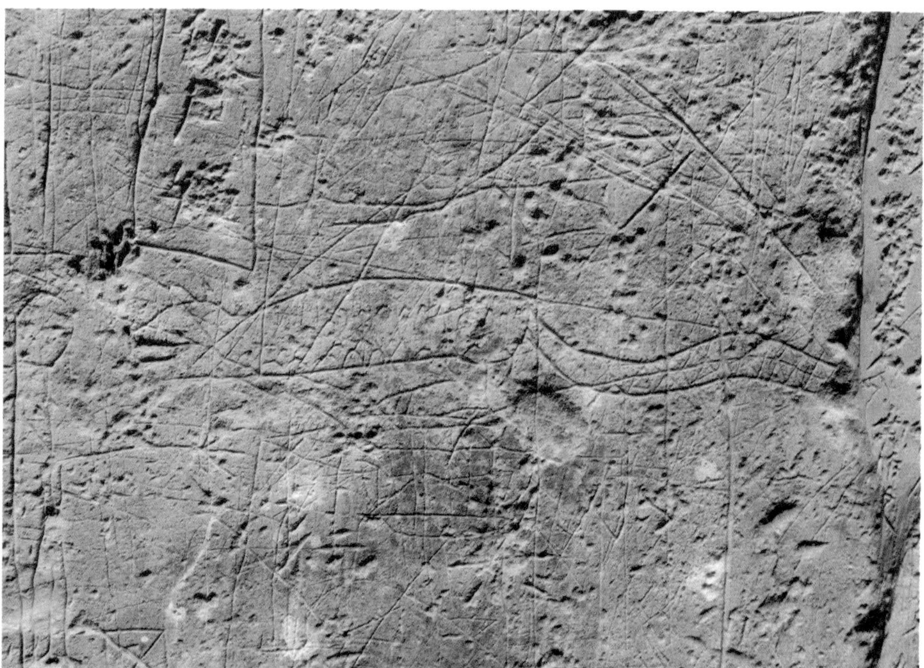

Photo 26. Panel A, thin-line engravings (A-TLE-72)

Photo 27. Panel A, thin-line engravings (A-TLE-74)

Photo 28. Panel A, thin-line engravings (A-TLE-76-1~78)

Photo 29. Panel A, thin-line engravings (A-TLE-89~96)

Photo 30. Panel A, thin-line engravings (A-TLE-106)

Photo 31. Panel A, thin-line engravings (A-TLE-117)

4) Textual Inscriptions

Textual inscriptions on Panel A number 221. Three of them are modern inscriptions consisting of names and dates. Most of the other 218 inscriptions are engraved with thin lines, though a few are chipped. There are more than 1,000 characters that were engraved during the Silla period. Above the procession scene on the lower left part are inscribed phrases indicating dates such as "Gaeseongsamnyeonmyeong (開成三年銘)," "Byeongsulmyeong (丙戌銘)," "Eulmimyeong (乙未銘)" and "Gyehaemyeong (癸亥銘)." Inside the boxes located on the lower right of the panel are inscribed the "main inscriptions." Below this box is the lower body of a person. Among the two types of inscriptions, the first inscribed is called "wonmyeong (原銘)" and the later inscribed is called "chumyeong (追銘)." Around the main inscriptions are some dates such as "Sinhaemyeong (辛亥銘)," some names of *hwarang* (the elite youth corps of Silla), and other inscriptions of unclear meaning.

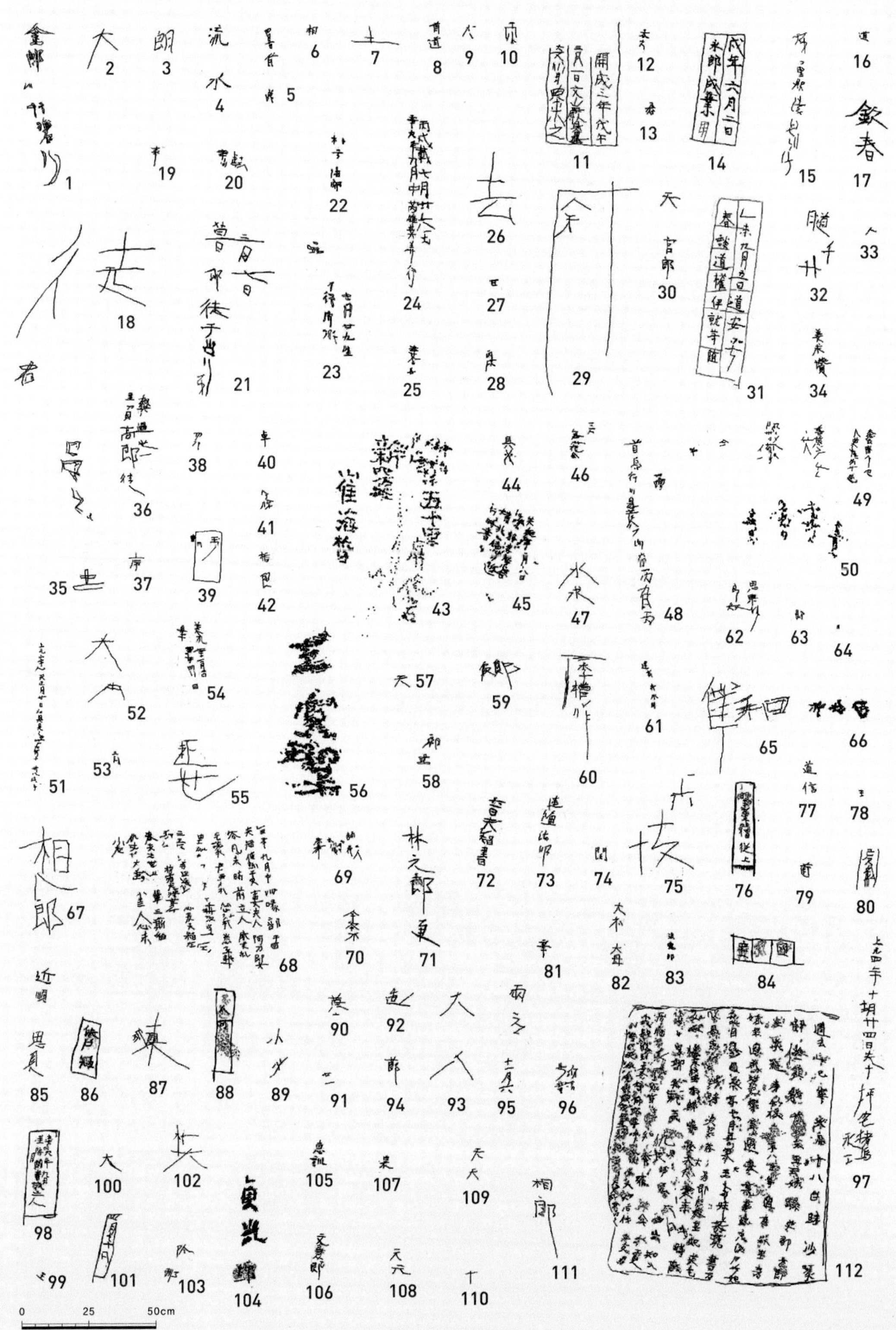

Fig. 19. A-TI, textual inscriptions 1 (1~112)

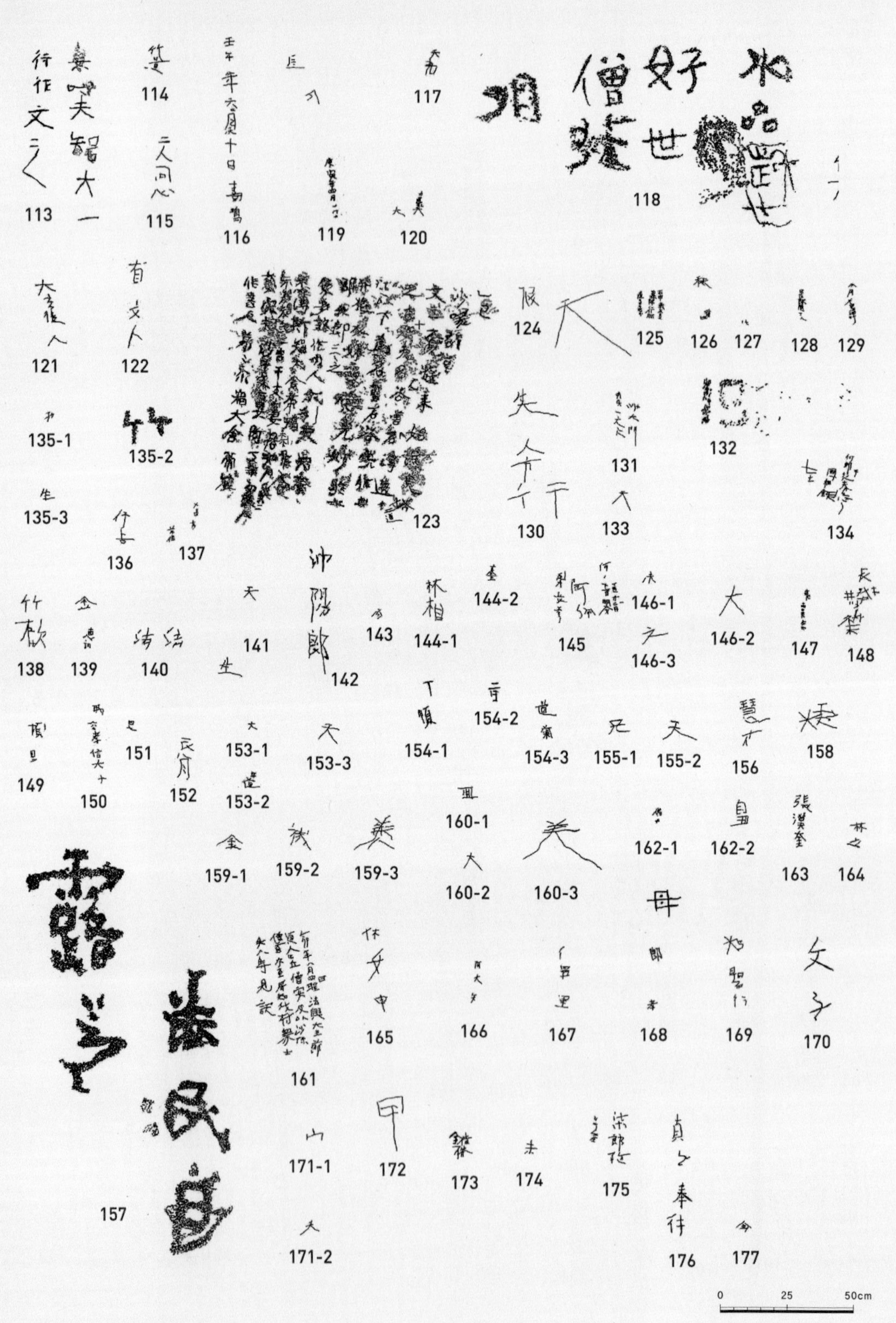

Fig. 20. A-TI, textual inscriptions 2 (113~177)

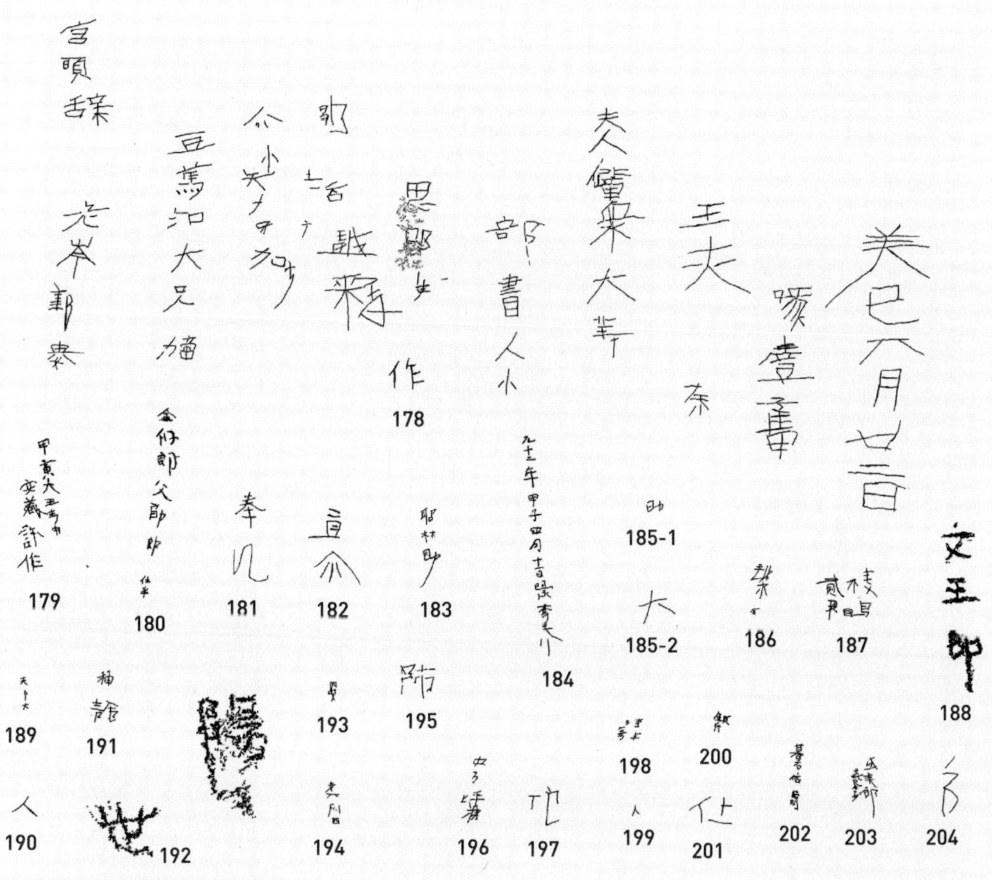

Fig. 21. A-TI, textual inscriptions 3 (178~204)

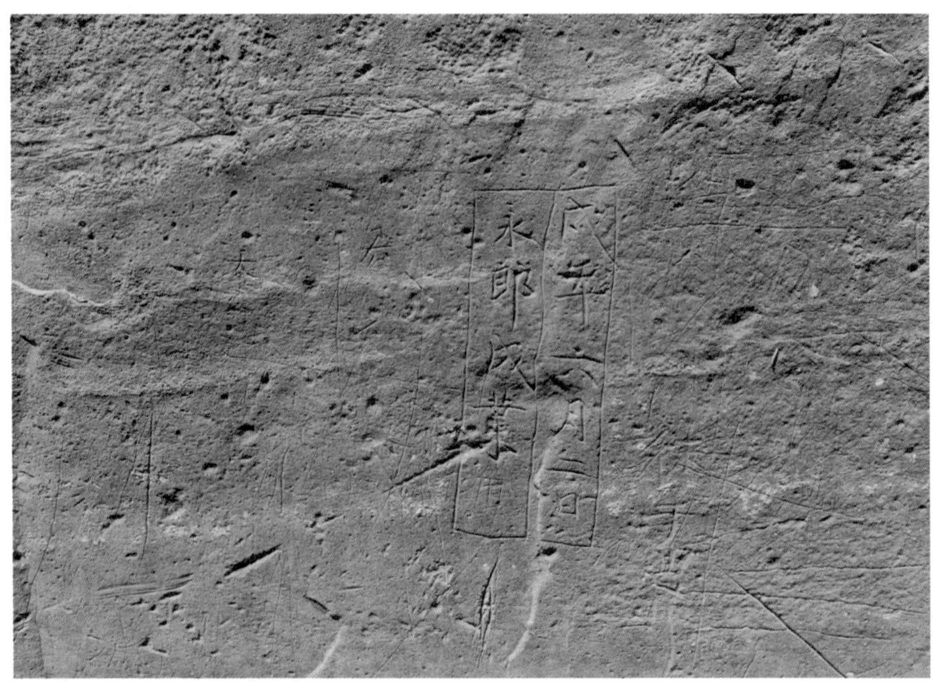

Photo 32. Panel A, textual inscriptions (A-TI-14)

Photo 33. Panel A, textual inscriptions (A-TI-31, 32)

Photo 34. Panel A, textual inscriptions (A-TI-42, 43)

Photo 35. Panel A, textual inscriptions (A-TI-45)

Photo 36. Panel A, textual inscriptions (A-TI-75~79, 84, 88)

Photo 37. Panel A, textual inscriptions (A-TI-98)

Photo 38. Panel A, textual inscriptions (A-TI-112, 123)

Photo 39. Panel A, textual inscriptions (A-TI-178)

5) Tools and Man-made Structures

The category of "tools" includes the bow (A-I-15) held by a person (A-I-14) and a parasol (A-TLE-23) held by a person. There are 18 man-made structures including boats, towers, and structures that look like watch towers, all engraved with thin lines (A-TLE-29, 30, 31, 39, 40, 41, 73-2, 76-3, 82, 89, 90, 91, 92, 108, 111, 112). There are also numerous thin lines concentrated on the lower right section of the panel. Based on the opinion of Jang Myeong-su, these lines are described as trees in this publication.

6) Unidentified Figures

This category consists of images that cannot be clearly identified. Some are not identifiable because of deterioration, whereas others, which are in good condition, are simply not identifiable. Currently, 107 of the total 777 figures are classified into the "unidentified" category (31 of A-I, 38 of A-II, 13 of A-TLE). There are also a number of unidentifiable figures on Panels B, C, and D.

Fig. 22 & Photo 40. Panel A, animals and humans (A-I-14, 16, 23, 24 / carnivora, humans)

Fig. 23 & Photo 41. Panel A, animals, humans, geometric patterns, thin-line engravings, and textual inscriptions (around A-I-169, A-TLE-77 / artiodactyla, carnivore, humans, circles, lozenges, textual inscriptions)

Fig. 24 & Photo 42. Panel A, animals and lozenges (A-I-71~76, A-II-4~8 / carnivora, artiodactyla, lozenges)

Fig. 25 & Photo 43. Panel A, waves, lozenges, and humans (A-II-16, 26, 46, 47 / waves, lozenges, face)

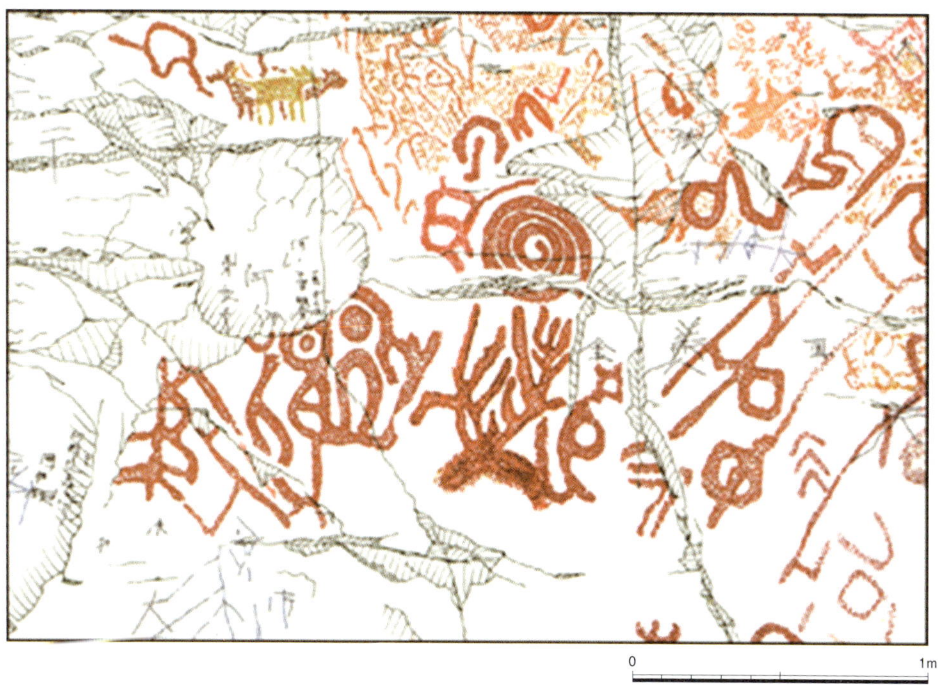

Fig. 26 & Photo 44. Panel A, unidentified figures and geometric patterns (A-II-89~96 / circles, lozenges)

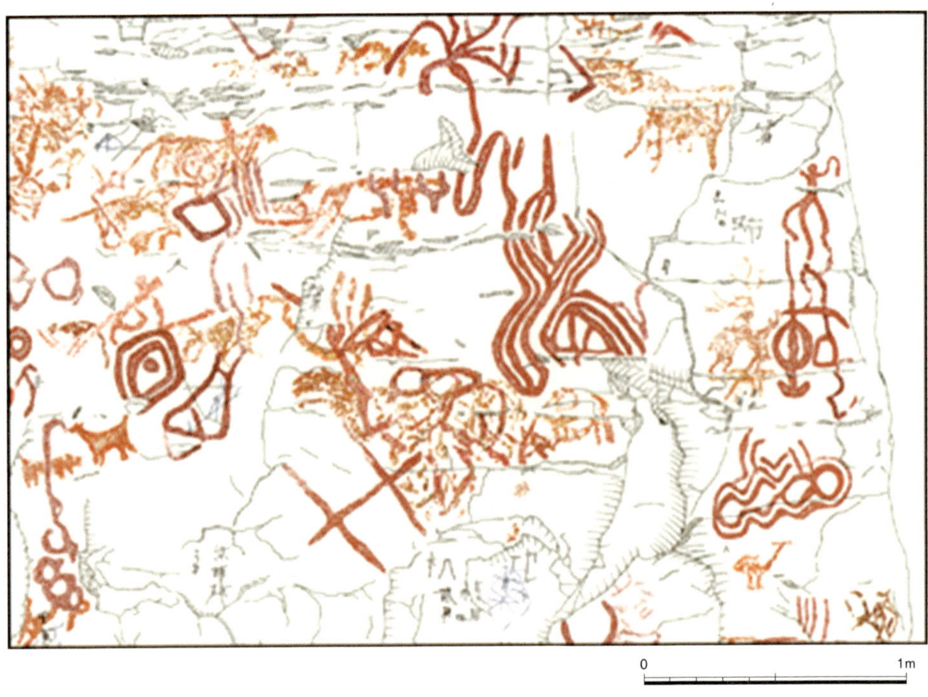

Fig. 27 & Photo 45. Panel A, animals, lozenges, and unidentified figures (A-I-202~211, A-II-118~130 / carnivora, lozenges)

Fig. 28 & Photo 46. Panel A, circles, lozenges, and humans (A-II-42~56 / circles, lozenges, face)

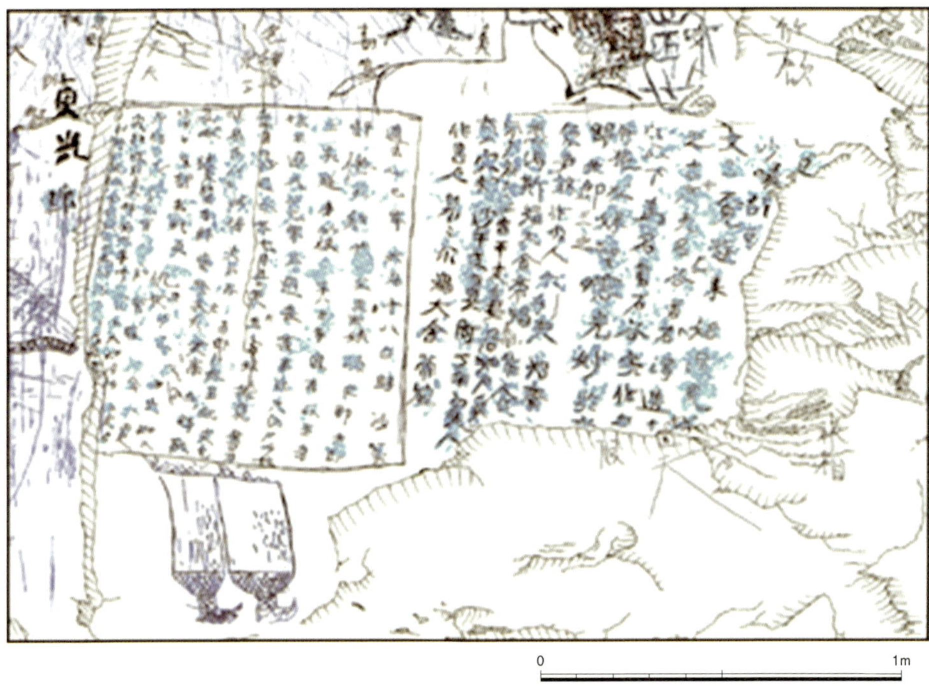

Fig. 29 & Photo 47. Panel A, thin-line engravings and textual inscriptions (A-TLE-74, A-TI-112, 123 / lower body of a human, textual inscriptions)

Fig. 30 & Photo 48. Panel A, thin-line engravings and textual inscriptions (A-TLE-32, A-TI-45)

Fig. 31 & Photo 49. Panel A, animals and humans in thin-line engravings (A-TLE-24~27 / artiodactyla, humans, thin-line engravings)

Fig. 32 & Photo 50. Panel A, animals and humans in thin-line engravings, and textual inscriptions (A-TLE-69, 71, 72, 75 (part), A-TI-75~79, 84, 86, 88 / birds, humans, dragon?, part of forest, textual inscriptions)

2. Panels B, C, D

1) Panel B

Panel B is located to the right of Panel A. The rock face is leaning forward and comprises two steps. On the rock face behind can be seen some traces of chipping. The chippings are generally shallow and deteriorated, so the figures are hard to identify. Ten of the figures have been classified into the "animal" category and five are unidentified. On the lower right part of the panel are three modern inscriptions.

Table 6. Classification of individual figures (Panel B)

Number	Group	Type	Length (mm)	Height (mm)	Carving technique
B-1	Unidentified	Unidentified	550	250	Silhouette chipping
B-2	Unidentified	Unidentified	780	250	Silhouette chipping
B-3	Unidentified	Unidentified	575	230	Silhouette chipping
B-4	Animals	Unidentified	480	340	Silhouette chipping
B-5	Animals	Unidentified	270	140	Silhouette chipping
B-6	Animals	Unidentified	155	130	Silhouette chipping
B-7	Animals	Carnivora	280	130	Silhouette chipping
B-8	Unidentified	Unidentified	110	120	Silhouette chipping
B-9	Animals	Artiodactyla / Unidentified	130	65	Silhouette chipping
B-10	Animals	Carnivora	150	30	Silhouette chipping
B-11	Animals	Unidentified	60	45	Silhouette chipping
B-12	Animals	Unidentified	240	130	Silhouette chipping
B-13-1	Animals	Unidentified	132	42	Silhouette chipping
B-13-2	Animals	Unidentified	414	179	Silhouette chipping
B-14	Unidentified	Unidentified	310	180	Thin-line engraving
B-15	Modern inscriptions		310	180	Silhouette chipping
B-16	Modern inscriptions		375	260	Thin-line engraving
B-17	Modern inscriptions		300	70	Silhouette chipping
Total	18 engravings				

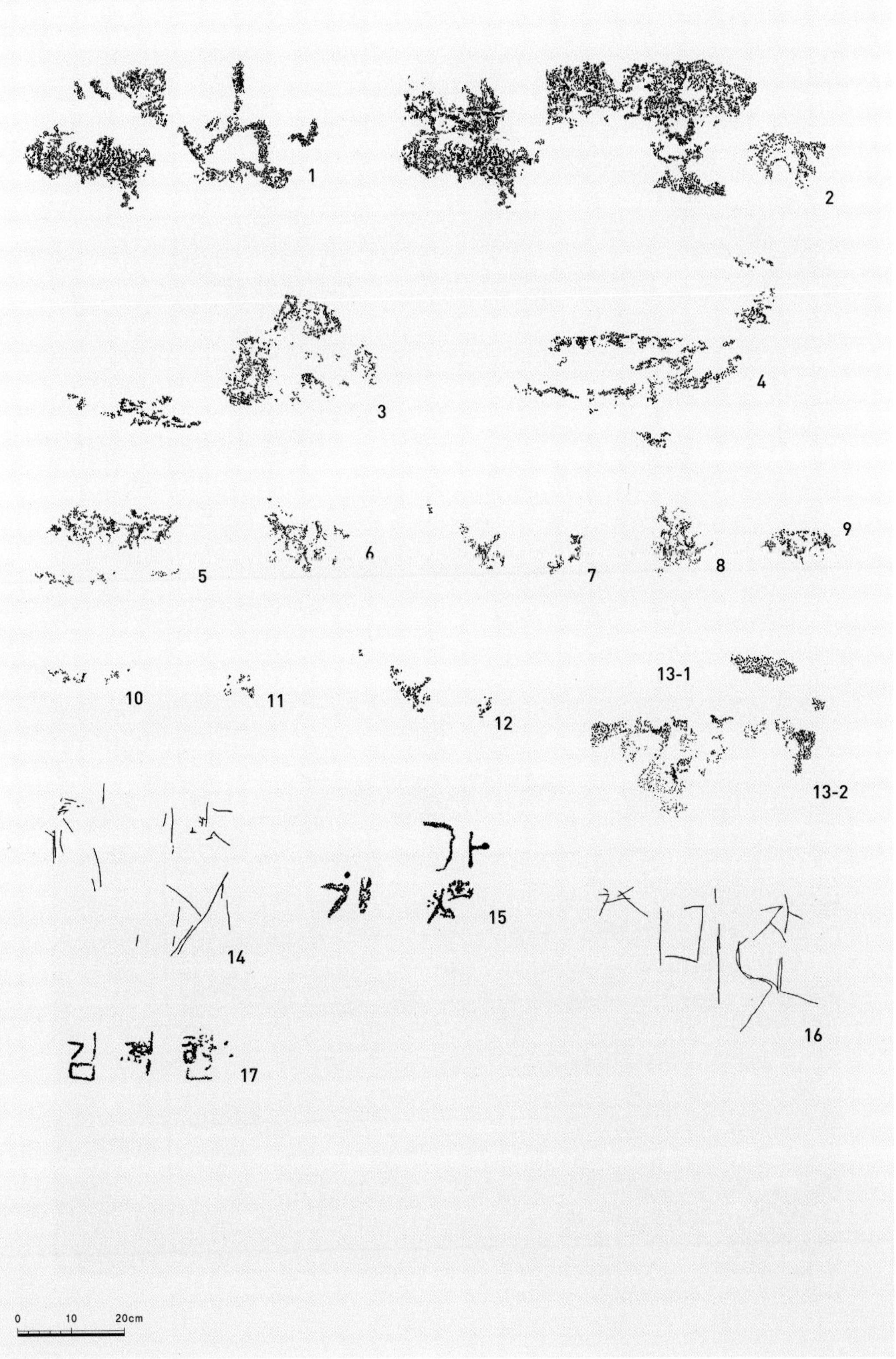

Fig. 33. Panel B, individual figures (1~17)

Photo 51. A complete view of panel B, the Cheonjeon-ri Petroglyphs

Photo 52. Panel B, unidentified figures (B-1~3)

2) Panel C

Panel C is connected to Panel B and located on the right side of Panel B. The rock face is severely damaged but shows some traces of shallow chipping. Some carvings can be identified as geometric patterns. Eleven modern inscriptions are on the lower part of the panel.

Table 7. Classification of individual figures (Panel C)

Number	Group	Type	Length (mm)	Height (mm)	Carving technique
C-1	Unidentified	Unidentified	1050	1020	Silhouette chipping
C-2	Unidentified	Unidentified	570	190	Silhouette chipping
C-3	Unidentified	Unidentified	770	420	Silhouette chipping
C-4	Unidentified	Unidentified	600	410	Silhouette chipping
C-5	Unidentified	Unidentified	860	750	Silhouette chipping
C-6	Unidentified	Unidentified	750	570	Silhouette chipping
C-7	Unidentified	Unidentified	480	350	Silhouette chipping
C-8	Unidentified	Unidentified	380	270	Silhouette chipping
C-9	Unidentified	Unidentified	590	360	Silhouette chipping
C-10	Geometric patterns	Checkered	900	110	Silhouette chipping
C-11	Geometric patterns	Unidentified	380	270	Silhouette chipping
C-12	Unidentified	Unidentified	690	570	Silhouette chipping
C-13	Geometric patterns	Unidentified	380	170	Silhouette chipping
C-14	Unidentified	Unidentified	280	400	Thin-line engraving
C-15	Unidentified	Unidentified	365	170	Thin-line engraving
C-16	Unidentified	Unidentified	1130	710	Thin-line engraving
C-17	Unidentified	Unidentified	400	190	Thin-line engraving
C-18	Modern inscriptions		75	130	Silhouette chipping
C-19	Modern inscriptions		180	430	Silhouette chipping
C-20	Modern inscriptions		130	160	Silhouette chipping
C-21	Modern inscriptions		150	150	Silhouette chipping
C-22	Modern inscriptions		120	170	Silhouette chipping
C-23	Modern inscriptions		170	150	Silhouette chipping
C-24	Modern inscriptions		210	85	Silhouette chipping
C-25	Modern inscriptions		300	120	Silhouette chipping

Number	Group	Type	Length (mm)	Height (mm)	Carving technique
C-26	Modern inscriptions		90	100	Silhouette chipping
C-27	Modern inscriptions		270	130	Silhouette chipping
C-28	Modern inscriptions		840	350	Thin-line engraving
Total	28 engravings				

Fig. 34. Panel C, individual figures 1 (1~9)

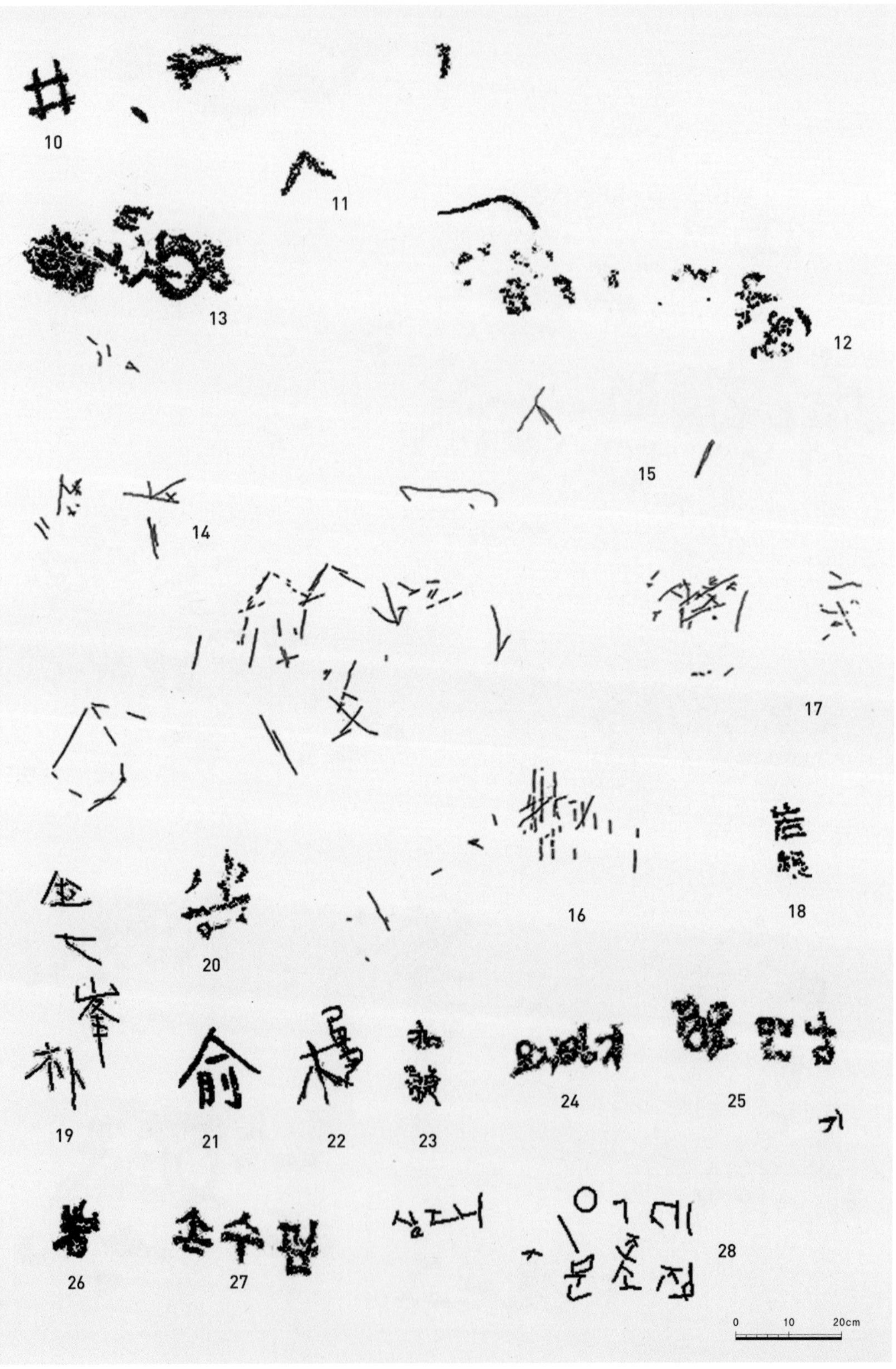

Fig. 35. Panel C, individual figures 2 (10~28)

Photo 53. A complete view of panel C, the Cheonjeon-ri Petroglyphs

Photo 54. Panel C, unidentified figures and geometric patterns (C-1~3, 9, 10, 14, 15, 18~21)

Photo 55. Panel C, geometric patterns (C-9, 10)

3) Panel D

Although the rock face is damaged, some geometric patterns on the upper left part of the panel as well as on the lower part are relatively clear. Among the 31 figures, 4 can be identified as double lozenges and waves. There also 2 mounted figures engraved with thin lines. The majority of engravings found on Panel D, however, are modern inscriptions and graffiti.

Table 8. Classification of individual figures (Panel D)

Number	Group	Type	Length (mm)	Height (mm)	Carving technique
D-1	Geometric patterns	Lozenges / Horizontal	580	290	Silhouette chipping
D-2	Geometric patterns	Circles / Linked circle	160	150	Silhouette chipping
D-3	Geometric patterns	Waves	300	230	Silhouette chipping
D-4	Geometric patterns	Waves	250	100	Silhouette chipping
D-5	Plants	Tree?	160	190	Thin-line engraving
D-6	Unidentified	Unidentified	170	120	Thin-line engraving

Number	Group	Type	Length (mm)	Height (mm)	Carving technique
D-7	Unidentified	Unidentified	240	400	Thin-line engraving
D-8	Unidentified	Unidentified	770	470	Thin-line engraving
D-9	Humans	Mounted figures	160	75	Thin-line engraving
D-10	Humans	Mounted figures?	490	300	Thin-line engraving
D-11	Unidentified	Unidentified	430	210	Thin-line engraving
D-12	Unidentified	Unidentified	530	90	Thin-line engraving
D-13	Group of thin lines	Unidentified	940	965	Thin-line engraving
D-14	Modern inscriptions		160	80	Silhouette chipping
D-15	Modern inscriptions		100	160	Silhouette chipping
D-16	Modern inscriptions		120	115	Silhouette chipping
D-17	Modern inscriptions		50	70	Silhouette chipping
D-18	Modern inscriptions		50	100	Thin-line engraving
D-19	Modern inscriptions		260	90	Silhouette chipping
D-20	Modern inscriptions		190	485	Silhouette chipping
D-21	Modern inscriptions		290	110	Silhouette chipping
D-22	Modern inscriptions		340	265	Silhouette chipping
D-23	Modern inscriptions		180	80	Silhouette chipping
D-24	Modern inscriptions		150	50	Silhouette chipping
D-25	Modern inscriptions		140	70	Silhouette chipping
D-26	Modern inscriptions		120	70	Silhouette chipping
D-27	Modern inscriptions		330	170	Silhouette chipping
D-28	Modern inscriptions		290	190	Silhouette chipping
D-29	Modern inscriptions		480	200	Silhouette chipping
D-30	Modern inscriptions		320	110	Silhouette chipping
D-31	Modern inscriptions		280	240	Silhouette chipping
Total	31 engravings				

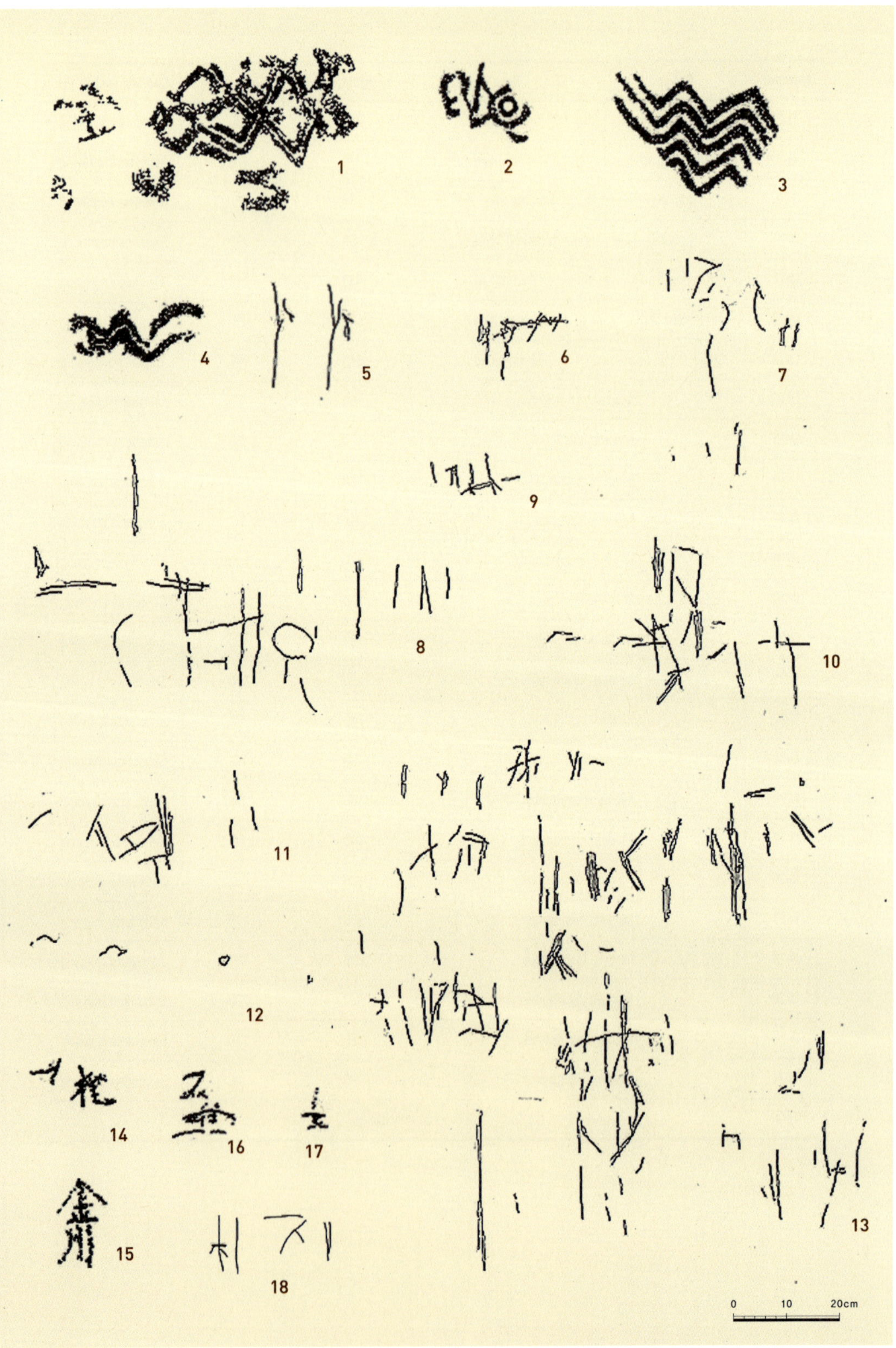

Fig. 36. Panel D, individual figures and inscriptions 1 (1~18)

Fig. 37. Panel D, individual figures and inscriptions 2 (19~31)

Photo 56. A complete view of panel D, the Cheonjeon-ri Petroglyphs

Photo 57. Panel D, geometric patterns (D-2, 3)

Photo 58. Panel D, modern inscriptions (D-21, 31)

Readings and Interpretations of the Textual Inscriptions

The following are the readings and interpretations of the textual inscriptions on Panel A, provided by Jang Myeong-su and Gang Jong-hun. The location numbers corresponds with the serial numbers of A-TI.

Loca-tion	Original inscription	Reading by Jang Myeong-su	Reading by Gang Jong-hun	Notes
1		金郎□行碧刂	金郎□行碧刂	"Geumrang□(金郎□) came here and engraved on the wall." 刂 appears to be the simplified character of 刻.
2		大	大	
3		朗	郎	朗 appears to be a different version of 郎.
4		流水	流水	
5		四月一日 首? 泮	四月一日 □ □	The last two characters are not identifiable. Possibly a codified signature.
6		相	相	
7		土	土	

Loca -tion	Original inscription	Reading by Jang Myeong-su	Reading by Gang Jong-hun	Notes
8		首道	首道	Not clear in meaning. Possibly a practice work.
9		大	大	
10		頁	□(頁?)	
11		開成三年戊午 三月一日文巖見□ 奇貨典來之	開成三年戊午 三月一日文巖見□ □□典來之	"On the first day of the third lunar month of 838, □□典 came to see the inscriptions on the rock."
12		呑之	□(呑?)之	Not clear in meaning
13			谷?	There was possibly another particle on top of 谷.
14		戌年六月二日 永郎成業 用 □(昔?)	戌年六月二日 永郎成業 □ □(共?)	"On the second day of sixth month of □戌 year, Yeonnang accomplished [what he was aiming at]." The missing character beneath 業 is possibly a codified signature.
15		□ □ 炽 淩 見 □ □	□ □ 里 娘? 徒 見 刻? 字?	"A group from □□ Village came to inscribe on the rock."

Loca-tion	Original inscription	Reading by Jang Myeong-su	Reading by Gang Jong-hun	Notes
16		道	道	
17		欽春	欽春	This is a name of Kim Yusin's younger brother. He was a *hwarang* under King Jinpyeong and a father of Bangul who was a hero of Hwangsanbeol Battle.
18		徒	徒	
19		事	事	
20		報書(畵?)	□□	Not identifiable
21		三月七日 暮郎徒于兌?	三月七日 暮郎徒于此?リ	"On the seventh day of the third month, the followers of Morang visited this place [and inscribed on the rock]." The character after 于 seems to be a different version of 此, considering the context.
22		朴兮法師	朴号(兮?)法師	The upper particle of the second character is either ロ or ソ.
23		七月卄九生 不行雨水 立…	七月卄九生 □行用?求? 立?…	"[Someone was] born on the 29th day of the seventh month. [He] did [something] and made his will to be used and sought for [good cause?]" The interpretation can be varied depending on the character before 行. The last character of the second line seems to be 求, with the horizontal stroke omitted.

Loca-tion	Original inscription	Reading by Jang Myeong-su	Reading by Gang Jong-hun	Notes
24		丙戌載七月卄六日 / 辛亥年九月中芮雄妻并行	丙戌載七月卄六日 / 辛亥年九月中芮雄妻并行	"On the 26th day of the seventh month of Byeongsul Year 746" / "In the ninth month of the Sinhae year (exact year not known), Yeung and his wife visited together." Between 744 and 758 year, the character 載 was used in the place of 年. Therefore, the Byeongsul year mentioned here is 746.
25		姜全長	□全長	Not clear in meaning
26		去	去	
27		日	日	
28		丙戌	丙戌	
29		人天	人天	
30		天 官郎	天 官郎	
31		乙未九月五日道安兮 春談道權伊就等隨	乙未九月五日道安号 春談道權伊就等隨	"On the fifth day of the Eulmi year, Doan summoned [his friends]. Chundam, Dogwn, Ichwi, and others followed."

Loca-tion	Original inscription	Reading by Jang Myeong-su	Reading by Gang Jong-hun	Notes
32		道 千 月 升	道 千 月 廿	Not clear in meaning
33		人	人	
34		姜求讚	姜求讚	
35		右呂之土	右呂之 土	Not clear in meaning
36		柳共遍世一 / 里負高郎徒	柳?共 遍世一 / 里負高郎徒	"Yu(?)gong wandered around the world." / "The group of Bugorang from □ Village."
37		康(庳?)	□(辰?)	
38		□	□	
39		玉(寺?) 月 / 書	玉(寺?) 月 / 書	Not clear in meaning
40		卓	卓	
41		條?	□	
42		相郎	椎(相?) □	

Loca-tion	Original inscription	Reading by Jang Myeong-su	Reading by Gang Jong-hun	Notes
43		竹花五十里屛風岩 新器(羅?) 崔海晳	□□五十里屛風?石 新器? 崔海晳	"The rocks spreading like a screen over 50 *li*" / "New vessel (talent)" / "Choe Haeseok" "New Vessel" is possibly a style name of Choe Haeseok
44		具□	具□	Not clear in meaning
45		癸亥年二月八日 沙喙□淩智小舍 婦非德刀遊 行時書	癸亥年二月八日 沙喙□淩智小舍 婦兆德刀遊 行時書	"On the eighth day of the second month, the wife of □*reungji* Sosa of Sadakbu leisurely visited here and wrote." 喙 is a character only used in Silla to indicate "rooster(*dak*)" in *Gyerim yusa* (鷄林類事).
46		三人 無心花余	三人 無心花余	"Three people" / "Aloof flowers" The last character 余 (*yeo*) is possibly exclamation mark indicating the Korean ending word.
47		水求	水求	Not clear in meaning. Possibly a practice work.
48		丙 / 首烏行川邊□□ 四育丙九月丙	丙 / 首烏行川邊共?徒? □□育?丙九月丙	"Suo visited the bank of the stream and group □□ ninth month of the Byeong□ year." Suo(首烏) means the leader of a crow, so it possibly means the leader of a *hwarang* group. The missing characters could mean "followed here to cultivate themselves" considering the context.

Loca-tion	Original inscription	Reading by Jang Myeong-su	Reading by Gang Jong-hun	Notes
49	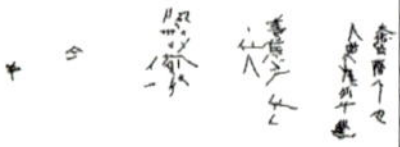	大德公隨下也 八□□□□巡 善焦□□ □八 □□□(化?)□ □ 羊	大德公隨下也 人菫?焦?□巡 善焦□□ □人 □□□□□ 今(仝?) 羊	"The followers of Master Daedeok cut the grass… The person who excelled in cutting the grass…"
50	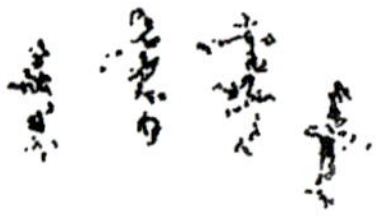	□寬? 裳恕心 叱(旨?)良(恨?)內 嘉□(壽?)	□□ □照□ 叱□內 分□□	Not clear in meaning
51	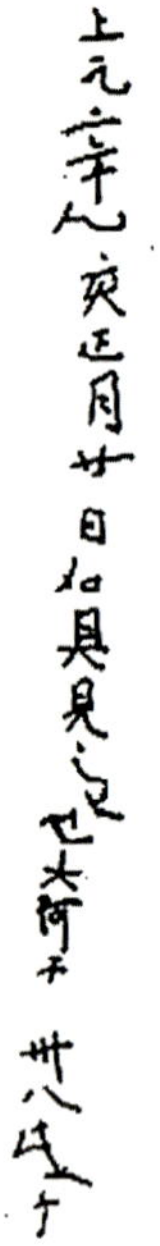	上元二年乙亥正月卄日加具見之匕也大阿干 卅八戌年	上元二年乙亥正月卄日加具見之匕也大阿干 卅八□□	"On the 20th day of the first month of the second reign year of Emperor Gaozong (Tang, China), the Eulhae year (675), *gagu* to see. Biya Daeagan." The meaning of *gagu* (加具) is not clear, but possibly means "go (*gada*)" written in *hyangchal* (vernacular script). The meaning of 卅八 is not clear. It possibly indicates the age of a person or a codified signature.
52		大□(本?)	大□	Not clear in meaning
53		三月	三月	

Loca -tion	Original inscription	Reading by Jang Myeong-su	Reading by Gang Jong-hun	Notes
54		癸亥年二月二日 辛酉年四月二日	癸亥年二月二日 辛酉年四月二日	
55		越世	越世	Possibly a name of a person, but it could just mean “transcending the world.”
56		王党?聖	王党?聖	Possibly a name of a person, but it could just mean “glorifying the king.”
57		天	天	
58		初立	初立	
59		鄭伋	鄭假	
60		李權(槽?)作	李權?作	
61	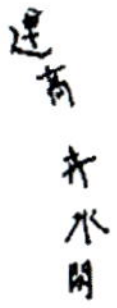	遑高卉水閃	遑?高卉水閑	Not clear in meaning

Loca-tion	Original inscription	Reading by Jang Myeong-su	Reading by Gang Jong-hun	Notes
62		思果沙 郎奴	思果沙 郎奴	Not clear in meaning. Possibly "a slave who adores Isarang."
63		郎	郎	
64		日	日	
65		崔知	崔知	Modern inscriptions
66		柳均百	柳均百	Modern inscriptions
67		想郎	想郎	
68	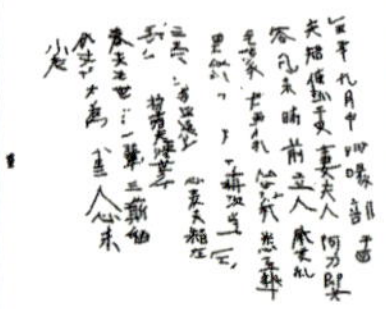	乙丑年九月中沙喙 部干西□ 夫智彼珎干支妻夫 人阿刀郎女 谷見來時前立人□ 女礼 乙□居…悉工栽 里□□□□午卄次□ □ 三壹□□迄□心羑夫 智在 □□ 杪宿夫□世丁 杪宿夫智世丁 春夫之世…輩三蕲枏 仇丈□大爲小王二人 心未 小老 云三(王?)	乙丑年九月中沙喙 部于西 夫智彼珎干支妻夫 人阿刀郎女 谷見來時前立人威? 女礼 兄喙?□迺?□□□悉 工赴? 里□□□□奔次逍?□ 三壹?□□迄□心麥夫 智在 王?□ 枕宿夫正汔世□ 春夫之世□一輩三蕲枏 仇丈□大爲 小王二人 心未 小老 云三(王?)	"In the ninth month of 445, Adorangnyeo, the wife of Pajinganji of Usebuji of Sadakbu visited the valley. The people ahead … when Simmaekbuji was a king … Chimsukbu … (meaning below here is not clear)."
69	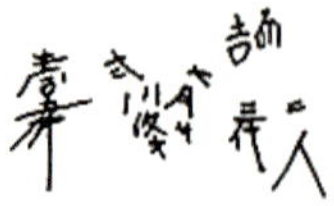	而 二人 吉 三代 七月廿 貳川條 壹□?	而 二人 吉 三代 七月廿 貳川條 壹□	Not clear in meaning

Loca -tion	Original inscription	Reading by Jang Myeong-su	Reading by Gang Jong-hun	Notes
70		仟岑水	仟?岑?水	Not clear in meaning
71		林元郎通	林元郎通?	The last character is possibly a codified signature.
72		昔夫智書	昔夫智書	
73		建通法師	建?通(遍?)法師	
74		閏	閏	
75		長技	長技	
76		□王七年僧徒上	日王七年僧徒上	
77		道信	道信	
78		王	王	

Loca-tion	Original inscription	Reading by Jang Myeong-su	Reading by Gang Jong-hun	Notes
79		道	道	
80		己欠□(越?)	己欠□(越?)	Not clear in meaning
81		辛	辛	
82		大不 大母	大不 大母	Not clear in meaning
83		法惠郎	法惠郎	
84		國□主	國□主?	
85		近順 思見	近順 思見	"Missing Geunsun."
86		伏戶智	伏戶智	
87		□(凍?, 湅?)	□	
88		□人可□	□人可□	

Loca-tion	Original inscription	Reading by Jang Myeong-su	Reading by Gang Jong-hun	Notes
89		小少	小少	
90		墓	墓	
91		廿一	廿一	
92		造	造	
93		大人	大人	
94		莭	節(莭?)	
95		兩及 十一月六日	兩交? 十一月六	
96		□(伓?)□(茘?) 馬(昜?)藝	□□(蕩?) □(昜?)□(藝?)	
97		上 元 四 年 十 十二 月 廿 四 日 夫 十 抨 宅 永 猪 工 塢	上 元 四 年 十 十二 月 廿 四 日 夫 十 抨 宅 永 猪 工 塢?	"On the 24th day of the 10th month of 677, [came] after the construction of the pig farm (?) at the residence of Busippyeong."

Loca-tion	Original inscription	Reading by Jang Myeong-su	Reading by Gang Jong-hun	Notes
98		辛亥年九月 圭陪朗者成三人 月	辛亥年九月 圭陪朗吉成三人 月	"In the ninth month of the Sinhae year, the three people Gyubae, Wollang, and Gilseong."
99		王	王	
100		大	大	
101		四月□(貳?)十日	四月□十日	The unreadable character is possibly a mistake.
102		朴大	朴大	
103		昤那	昤?那	Not clear in meaning
104		貞光郞	貞光郞	
105		惠訓	惠訓	
106		文僉郞	文僉郞	
107		白衣	白衣	

Loca-tion	Original inscription	Reading by Jang Myeong-su	Reading by Gang Jong-hun	Notes
108		元元	元元	
109		天天	天天	
110		十	十	
111		相郎	相郎	
112	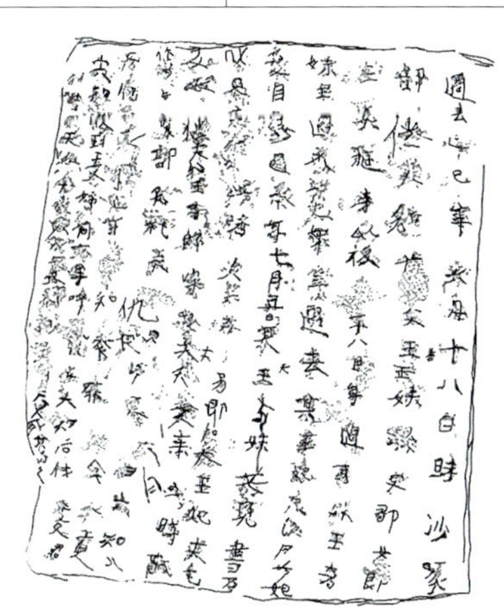	過去乙巳年六月十八日昧沙喙 善 部徙夫知葛文王妹於史鄒安郎 王共遊來此後□年八巳年過去妹王考 妹王過人丁巳年王過去其王妃只沒尸兮妃 天 愛自思己未年七月三日其王与妹共見書石 叱見來谷此時共三來 另卽知太王妃夫乞 夫 支妃徙夫知王子郎深□夫知共來此時酉咸 作功臣喙部知礼夫知沙干支 泊六知 仇良 居伐干支礼□丁乙尒知奈麻作食人眞 宍智波珎干支婦何女牟呼夫人尒夫知居伐干支婦 一利等次夫人居礼次□干支郡沙爻功夫人分共作之	過去乙巳年六月十八日昧沙喙 善 部徙夫知葛文王王妹於史鄒女郎 王共遊來以後□□十八□□過□妹王考 妹王過人丁巳年王過去其王妃只沒尸兮妃 天 愛自思己未年七月三日其王与妹共見書石 叱見來谷此時共王來 另卽知太王妃夫乞? 夫 支妃徙夫知王子郎深□夫知共來此?時□ 作□□喙部□礼夫知□干支 □六知 仇良 居伐干支□乙□□知奈麻□食人眞 宍智波珎干支婦何□牟呼夫人□夫知居伐 干支婦 □利等□夫人□□□□干支□沙□□夫人分 共作之	

Loca-tion	Original inscription	Reading by Jang Myeong-su	Reading by Gang Jong-hun	Notes
112	"In the early morning of the eighteenth day of the sixth lunar month of the Eulsa year (乙巳, 525), King Eobuji Galmun (徙夫知 葛文王) of Sadakbu (沙喙部) and his sister, Queen Eosachu yeorang (於史鄒 女郎), visited [this place] together. Eight years has passed since then. Thinking of the king's sister, she has become a person of the past [passed away]. Then in the Jeongsa year (丁巳, 536), the king passed away. Because the queen missed him so much, on the third day of the seventh month of the Gimi year (己未, 539), she came to see the Seoseok (書石, lettered stone) in the valley where the king and his sister used to come. The queen of the Great King Yeongjeukji (另卽知), Bugeoljibi (夫乞支妃), and Prince Sabuji Sim□buji (徙夫知 深□夫知), the son of King Sabuji came together. The one who [conducted the ritual] was □raebuji □ganji (□礼夫知 □干支), □yukji (□六知) Geobeolganji (居伐干支) from Dakbu (喙部, and □eul□□ji Nama (□乙□□知奈麻). The cooks were Lady A□moho (何□牟呼), wife of Jinyukji Pajinganji (眞肉知波珍干支); Lady □lideung□ (□利等□), wife of □buji Geobeolganji (□夫知 居伐干支); and Lady Sa□□ (沙□□), wife of □□□□ Ganji (□□□□干支)." This long inscription is related to 123 and is commonly called "Wonmyeong (original inscription)." 123 is called "Chumyeong (following inscription)." Some characters are not clear. The two readings by Jang and Gang present the characters that are considered to be valid based on the context of the text and the related historical documents.			
113		六叶夫智大一 行作文之	六叶夫智大一 行作文之	"Yukyeopbuji Daeil ... came and wrote this."
114		竹道	竹道	
115		二人同心	二人同心	

Loca -tion	Original inscription	Reading by Jang Myeong-su	Reading by Gang Jong-hun	Notes
116		壬 午 年 口 六 沃 月 十 日 壽 瑦	壬 午 年 口 六 沃 月 十 日 壽? 瑦?	"On the 10th day of the sixth month of the Imo year, Suo (?)" The unreadable character and the character 口 and 沃 seem to be modern graffiti.
117		夭□ / □(今?) / □(追?, 進?)	夭□ / □(分?) / □(進?)	
118		水品罡?世 好世 僧苑 明	水品罡世 好世 僧苑 明?	"Supum, Gangse, Hose, Monk Wonmyeong" Supum was a prime minister (*sangdaedeung*) during the reign of Queen Jinpyeong and Hose was a *hwarang* at that time.
119		庚寅年四月□日	庚寅年四月□日	
120		力弔苑天 / 大	力君?苑天 / 大	Not clear in meaning
121		大玄徒人	大玄徒人	

<table>
<tr><th>Loca
-tion</th><th>Original inscription</th><th>Reading by
Jang Myeong-su</th><th>Reading by
Gang Jong-hun</th><th>Notes</th></tr>
<tr><td>122</td><td>有
文
人</td><td>有文人</td><td>有文人</td><td></td></tr>
<tr><td rowspan="3">123</td><td colspan="4">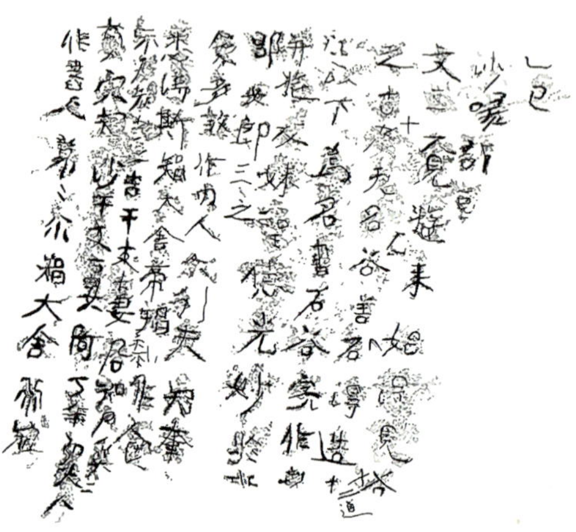</td></tr>
<tr><td colspan="2">乙巳…
沙喙部□
文王覓遊來始淂見谷
十 乙 十二道
之古谷无名谷善石淂造□(十?)
□□下爲名書石谷字作□
幷遊友妹□德光妙於史
鄒安郎三之
□多煞作功人介利夫智奈
悉淂斯智大舍帝智□作食□
榮知智壹吉干支妻居知尸奚□
眞宍智沙干支妻阿兮牟弘夫人
作書人慕ː介智大舍帝智</td><td colspan="2">乙巳…
沙喙部葛…
文王覓遊來始得見谷
十 乙 十二道
之古□(來?)无名谷善石得造□(書?)
記?以下爲名書石谷字作□(之?)
幷遊友妹聖德光妙於史
鄒女郎王之
□多煞作□(功?)人介利夫智奈…
悉得斯智大舍帝智□作食…
□□智壹?吉干支妻□(居?)知尸奚夫?…
□(眞?)宍智沙干支妻阿丂?牟弘夫人
作書人慕ː介智大舍帝智</td></tr>
<tr><td colspan="4">"In the Eulsa year (乙巳, 525), King Galmun from the district of Sadakbu (沙喙部) and his entourage visited the valley. It was their first time visiting this place. The valley was very old, but it did not have a name. Therefore, he named the valley "Seoseokgok" (書石谷, "valley of the lettered stone") and inscribed characters on the rock. Galmun was accompanied by his sister, Princess Eosachu yeorang (於史鄒 女郎) whose divine virtue was shimmering like light.
Those who (meaning is not clear) were Iribuji Na(ma)(介利夫知 奈麻), and Sildeuksaji Daesajaeji (悉淂斯知 大舍帝智). Those who cooked were Lady □geojisihye (居知尸奚),</td></tr>
</table>

Loca-tion	Original inscription	Reading by Jang Myeong-su	Reading by Gang Jong-hun	Notes
123	wife of □ji Il?gilganji (□智 壹?吉干支) and Lady Ahye?mohong (阿兮?牟弘), wife of □jin?yukji Saganji (□眞?肉知 沙干支). The one who composed this inscription was Momoyiji Daesajaeji (慕慕尒智 大舍帝智)." The lower part of the inscription fell off. The first and the second line are in extremely bad condition. Most likely, after the "Eulsa year" of the first line, the day and the month were originally recorded. Supposedly, "King Sabuji Galmun" was carved after "King Galmun of Sabuji." The third character of the fourth line has been read as 谷, but it looks more like 來, which also fits the context better. The last character of the fourth line looks like 十 because only the upper part of the character remains. Considering that the first character of the fifth line is close to 記, it is more likely that the original character was 書. All that remains in the last character of the fifth line is its upper part, but considering the context, it looks like the ending word 之. There has been controversy about the reading of the fifth and the sixth characters of the sixth line, but this research clarified that they are 聖德. It also identified the second character of the seventh line, 女, and the fourth character of the seventh line, 王. The last character of the eighth line seems to be a mistake of the character 奈 and the missing character below is supposedly 麻, considering the context. The last character of the tenth line seems to be 夫, and the missing character below is 人, also considering the context. The sign in the last line means 疊, used for the repetition of the previous character.			
124		天 / 限	天 / 假	
125		丙申載五月七 慕郎行賦(賑?) 道谷造作	丙申載五月七 慕郎行賑(賦?) 道谷造刂(忄?)	"On the seventh day of the fifth month of 756, Morang wrote on the way to Guhyul."
126		秼(頏?)曰	秼 頏?曰	Not clear in meaning
127		□(七?)	□(七?)	
128		柒陵郎隨三人	柒陵郎隨三人	"Three people after Chilleungrang"

Loca -tion	Original inscription	Reading by Jang Myeong-su	Reading by Gang Jong-hun	Notes
129		今月大□(龜?) 溫叮	今月大臣? 龜?叮	“This month, Minister Gwijeong [came].”
130		先人卞行	先人卞行	Not clear in meaning. The readable characters can be read as “ancestors acted hastily,” but the phrase is not meaningful or worth recording.
131		□大門 丸失一元□	□大門 □□一元□	Not clear in meaning
132		19□□	19□□	Modern inscriptions
133		天	天	
134		□(干?) 何朗徒夫□□ □(回?)相銀 七十一	□(干?) 何郞徒夫□□ □相□ 七十一	Not clear in meaning
135-1 /-2/-3		□(孤?) / 竹 / 生	□(孤?) / 竹 / 生	
136		行吉	行吉	
137		メ吊□(左?) 羊佳	メ吊?□(左?) 羊佳	Not clear in meaning

Loca -tion	Original inscription	Reading by Jang Myeong-su	Reading by Gang Jong-hun	Notes
138		竹歡	竹歡?	
139		金 惠訓	金 惠訓	
140		法法	法法	Probably a practice work
141-1 /-2		天 / 生	天 / 生	
142		沖陽郎	沖陽郎	
143		□(均?)	□	
144-1 /-2		林相 / 京全□(上?)	林相 / 京全上?	Not clear in meaning
145		一 丁酉十二月 何 十七日明□ 阿佩 □(梨?)長芸?	一 丁酉廿二月 何十七日明□ 阿佩 □長□	"On the 17th day of the twelfth month of the Jeongyu year"
146-1 /-2/-3		未 / 大 / 之	未 / 大 / 之	Possibly a practice work
147		蒽 十四日共全巾	慕 十四日共全巾	Not clear in meaning

Loca-tion	Original inscription	Reading by Jang Myeong-su	Reading by Gang Jong-hun	Notes
148		□ 戊戌年□ 共□	□ □□□□ □□□	Possibly a practice work
149		項 目二	項 目二	Possibly a practice work
150		馬谷孝信大子	馬谷孝信大子	
151		日七	日七(皂?)	
152		辰八月	辰八月	
153-1 /-2/-3		大 / 立道 / 天	大 / □(立?)道 / 天	
154-1 /-2/-3		丁順 / 二日 / 道義	丁順 / 二日 / 道業?	Possibly a practice work
155-1 /-2		兄 / 天	兄 / 天	
156		慧□	慧花?	Possibly a practice work
157		法民良(郎?) 露芝	法民郎? 露□	法民 has the same pronunciation with 法敏, the name of King Munmu. It is worth an attention.

Loca-tion	Original inscription	Reading by Jang Myeong-su	Reading by Gang Jong-hun	Notes
158		妖	□(妖?)	Possibly a practice work
159-1/-2/-3		金 / □成 / 癸	金 / □ / □	Possibly a practice work
160-1/-2/-3		囲 / 大 / 癸	囲 / 大 / 癸	Possibly a practice work
161		日 乙卯年八月四聖 法興大王節 道人比丘僧安 及以沙弥 僧首乃至居知 伐村衆士 □人等見記	日 乙卯年八月四聖 法興大王節 道人比丘僧安 及以沙弥 僧首乃至居知 伐村衆士 六?人等見記	"On the fourth day of the eighth month of 535, during the reign of King Beopeung the Divine, monk Angeubi, boy monk Sunaeji and Geoji, and six people from Beolchon Village saw and recorded." The first character of the last line is not clear. It is possibly a revision of the character 人, which was mistakenly carved in the place of 六.
162-1/-2		偖曰 / 自丑	偖曰 / 自丑	
163		張漢奎	張漢奎	
164		林之	林之	
165		休女申	休女申	
166		阿大矢	阿大知?	
167		□置里	亻置里	Possibly a practice work

Loca-tion	Original inscription	Reading by Jang Myeong-su	Reading by Gang Jong-hun	Notes
168		郎 / 孝 / 母	郎 / 孝 / 母	Possibly a practice work
169		奶碧?行	奶?碧?行	Possibly a practice work
170		父子	父子	Possibly a practice work
171-1 /-2		宀 / 夫	宀 / 夫	Possibly a practice work
172		甲	甲	Possibly a practice work
173		金 偖倄	金 佶(偖?)倄	Possibly a practice work
174		未	未	
175		柒郎隨 □□□□	柒郎隨 □□□□	
176		貞兮奉行	貞□(兮?)奉行	
177		金	金	

Loca-tion	Original inscription	Reading by Jang Myeong-su	Reading by Gang Jong-hun	Notes
178		癸巳六月廿二日 喙壹奮 王夫□…奈 夫人輩衆大等… 部書人小… 思郎□□作 鄒□越?釋? 尒小知大兄旛 豆篤知大兄加少 宮頭辭…老岑邽妻?	癸巳六月廿二日 喙壹奮 王夫□…奈 夫人輩衆大等… 部書人小… 思郎女□作 鄒?呑越?釋? 尒小知大兄加 豆篤知大兄加 宮頭辭…老岑邽?妻?	"On the 22nd day of the sixth month of 514, Ilbun from Dakbu (meaning of the rest not known)"
179		甲寅大王寺中 安藏許作	甲寅大王寺中 安藏許作	"In the Gabin year, Anjang from the Daewang Temple allowed to write this."
180		金仍(?)郎 夫師郎 仕半	金仍?郎 父師郎 仕半	

Loca -tion	Original inscription	Reading by Jang Myeong-su	Reading by Gang Jong-hun	Notes
181		奉氿	奉氿?	
182		亘尒	亘?尒	
183		□(聖?, 聒?)林助	□(聖?, 聒?)林助	
184		元十二年甲子四月十一日喙奪?毛刂	元十二年甲子四月十一日喙奪?毛刂	"On the 11th day of the fourth month of the Gapja year, the twelfth year of □won, Junmo from Dakbu inscribed."
185-1 /-2		助 / 大	助(叻?) / 大	Possibly a practice work
186		□(越?)來(求?) 金	□(越?)來(求?) 金	Possibly a practice work
187		積(棱?)賜 机貳□	積(棱?)賜 机貳□	Possibly a practice work

Loca -tion	Original inscription	Reading by Jang Myeong-su	Reading by Gang Jong-hun	Notes
188		文王郎	文王郎	
189		天卜大	天卜大	
190		人	人	
191		神詥(話?)	神話(詥?)	
192		陽世	陽世	
193		內安	內安	Possibly a practice work
194	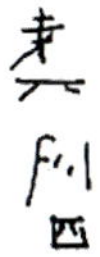	年六月四	年?六月?四	Possibly a practice work
195		□?	陁?	
196	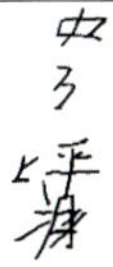	中之坪泂	中之?坪泂	Possibly a practice work

Loca-tion	Original inscription	Reading by Jang Myeong-su	Reading by Gang Jong-hun	Notes
197		□	□	Possibly a practice work
198		□主 土□	□主 土□	Possibly a practice work
199		人	人	
200		銀行	銀行	
201		仕	仕	
202		暮石信嗢別	暮石信嗢別	
203		成年郎 尒此□□□	成年郎 尒此□□□	Possibly a practice work
204		□?	阝?	Possibly a practice work

Summary

The Cheonjeon-ri Petroglyphs are located in Cheonjeon-ri, Dudong-myeon, Ulju-gun, Ulsan Metropolitan City. Cheonjeon-ri used to belong to the Nam-myeon and Oenam-myeon townships of Gyeongju before it was incorporated into Dobuk-myeon township of Ulsan-bu in 1905 (42nd year of the reign of King Gojong). In the Three Kingdoms period, this region belonged to Goheo-bu, one of the six divisions of Silla. From 32 BCE (9th year of the reign of Yuri Isageum of Silla) to 940 (23rd year of the reign of King Taejo of Goryeo), it was part of Saryang-bu of Gyeongju. The distance between the Cheonjeon-ri Petroglyphs to the site of the Silla palace Wolseong (Moon Palace) in Gyeongju by way of Chari-deul Field is 25 kilometers, which is a relatively short distance.

There are a considerable number of archaeological and historic sites such as Bronze Age sites, Three Kingdoms tombs, and Unified Silla temple sites throughout the flat land and low hills between Eonyang and Gyeongju, which means that this area was well-known to the prehistoric and ancient people. Some important sites are the 4th century to 7th century Chari Tomb Complex built on the low hills of the Chari-deul Field, the Hasamjeong Tomb Complex where over 1,000 tombs dating from the 3rd century to the 6th century are found. Along with the thin line engravings and the textual inscriptions of the Cheonjeon-ri Petroglyphs, these sites contribute to the value of this area as a living and cultural space for ancient people.

The Cheonjeon-ri Petrolyphs comprise various figures and textual inscriptions of different subjects, styles, and techniques. The figures on the main rock panel include silhouettes of human figures and animals engraved with shallow pecking, geometric patterns produced by pecking outlines and grinding, later figures engraved with sharp metal tools, and numerous short and long textual inscriptions. These are all important historic and artistic sources that contribute to understanding the society and culture of early Korea.

This report divided the main rock panel of Cheonjeon-ri into Panel A, Panel B, Panel C, and Panel D. Panel A, which is the main panel, is then divided into A-I (figures in silhouette, pecked), A-II (geometric patterns, outline-pecked), A-TLE (thin-line engravings), and A-TI (textual inscriptions). The figures on the other panels are classified using the same methodology. The total 777 figures and inscriptions are identified, including 253 textual inscriptions (32%), 226 animal figures (29%), 93 geometric patterns (12%), 61 human figures (8%), 21 tools and man-made structures (3%), and 16 plants (2%). The other 107 images are unidentifiable.

There were some difficulties in individualizing each figure as some figures, such as geometric patterns, are linked with each other or grouped together. Despite the difficulties, this report tries to provide serial numbers to all the identifiable and separable figures in order to facilitate future studies.

So far, many different opinions about the iconography, subject, and date of the Cheonjeon-ri Petroglyphs have been suggested. As for the production date, both Neolithic and Bronze Age dates have been suggested. The concentric circles and the double lozenges are interpreted in relation to earth goddess worship and rituals, and the figures and inscriptions carved with thin lines are understood as works of the Unified Silla period.

Bibliography

Choe, Geunyeon. 1985. "Hanguk seonsa godaein-ui taeyang sungbae sasang-ui ilcheukmyeon," *Cheon Gwanu seonsaeng hwallyeok ginyeom hanguk sahak nonchong.*

Choe, Gwangsik. 2010. "Cheonjeon-ri amgakhwa balgyeon-ui yeoksajeok uiui," *Cheonjeon-ri amgakhwa balgyeon 40-junyeon ginyeom haksul daehoe nonmunjip.*

Cultural Heritage Administration of Korea. 2012. *Daegokcheon amgakhwa gun bojon haksuljosa yeongu yongyeok.*

E, Anati. 2000. "Seonsa bawigeurim-ui chulhyeon baegyeong-gwa uimi," *Ulsan amgakhwa balgyeon 30-junyeon ginyeom amgakhwa gukje haksul daehoe nonmunjip*, Seoul Arts Center, Ulsan Metropolitan City.

Gang, Simhye. 2010. "Cheonjeon-ri amgakhwa-ui gihahakjeok munnyang-gwa seonsamisul," *Cheonjeon-ri amgakhwa balgyeon 40-junyeon ginyeom haksul daehoe nonmunjip.*

Gang, Yeonggyeong. 2003. "Baikal jiyeok-ui syameon bawiwa syameon uirye," *Hanguk amgakhwa yeongu 4.*

Gwon, Odae. 2005. "Bukmi jiyeok Kokopelli amgakhwa-wa Ulsan jiyeok amgakhwa-ui sanggwanseong," *Hanguk amgakhwa yeongu 6.*

Hanguk seonsamisul yeonguso. 2003. *Cheonjeon-ri gakseok silcheuk josa bogoseo*, Ulsan Metropolitan City.

Heo, Eonuk. 2000. "Ulsan amgakhwa-ui munhwa gwangwang jawon gaebal munje," *Ulsan amgakhwa balgyeon 30-junyeon ginyeom amgakhwa gukje haksul daehoe nonmunjip*, Seoul Arts Center, Ulsan Metropolitan City.

Heo, Gwon. 2010. "Ulsan amgakhwa jiyeok-ui segye yusan deungjae chujin-ui hyeonhwang-gwa gwaje," *Cheonjeon-ri amgakhwa balgyeon 40-junyeon ginyeom haksul daehoe nonmunjip.*

Hwang, Suyeong and Mun, Myeongdae. 1984. *Bangudae ambyeok jogak*, Dongguk University.

Hwang, Yonghun. 1975. "Hanbando seonsa sidae amgak-ui jejakgibeop-gwa hyeongsik bullyu," *Gogomisul 127.*

__________. 1977. "Hanguk seonsa amgakhwa yeongu," Ph.D. Dissertation, Kyunghee University.

__________. 1987. *Dongbuk asia-ui amgakhwa*, Seoul: Mineumsa.

Jang, Myeongsu. 1996. "Hanguk amgakhwa-ui pyeonnyeon," *Hanguk-ui amgakhwa,* Hanguk yeoksa minsok hakhoe, Hangilsa.

__________. 1997. "Amgakhwa-e natanan seongsinang moseup," *Gomunhwa 50*, Hanguk daehak bakmulgwan hyeophoe.

__________. 1997. "Hanguk amgakhwa-ui pyeonnyeon," *Hanguk-ui amgakhwa*, Hanguk yeoksa minsok hakhoe, Hangilsa.

__________. 1999. "Amgakhwa-reul tonghaeseo bon urinara seonsa-indeurui sinang sayu," *Hanguk amgakhwa yeongu 1.*

__________. 1999. "Ulju Daegok-ri Bangudae amgakhwa-e natanan sinang uisik," *Ulsan yeongu 1.*

__________. 2001. "Hanguk amgakhwa-ui munhwasang-e daehan yeongu," Ph.D. Dissertation, Inha University.

__________. 2001. "Ulsan amgakhwa-ui munhwasang-e daehan yeongu: sinang-ui jeongae yangsang-eul jungsim-euro," Ph.D. Dissertation, Inha University.

__________. 2003. "Munhwajae-e daehan insik-gwa amgakhwa-ui bojon," *Hanguk amgakhwa yeongu 4.*

__________. 2004. "Cheonjeon-ri amgakhwa-ui hyeongsang bunseok 1," *Hakye-yeongu 5, 6.*

__________. 2007. "Hanguk amgakhwa-ui hyeongsik bullyu-wa munhwa teukseong," *Hanguk amgakhwa yeongu 10.*

Jang, Seokho. 1986. "Bangudae amgakhwa-ui johyeong-seong yeongu," Master Dissertation, Keimyung University.

__________. 1991. "Ulsan Cheonjeon-ri seoseok gakhwa yeongu," *Yesul munhwa 4*, Institute for Arts and Culture Research, Keimyung University.

__________. 2000. "Daegok-ri amgakhwa-ui hyeongsang bunseok-gwa yangsik bigyo," *Ulsan amgakhwa balgyeon 30-junyeon ginyeom amgakhwa gukje haksul daehoe nonmunjip*, Seoul Arts Center, Ulsan Metropolitan City.

Jeon, Hotae. 1996. "Ulju Daegok-ri, Cheonjeon-ri amgakhwa," *Hanguk-ui amgakhwa*, Hanguk yeoksa minsok hakhoe, Hangilsa.

__________. 1999. "Ulju Cheonjeon-ri seoseok seseon gakhwa yeongu," *Ulsan yeongu 1*, Museum of University of Ulsan.

Jeon, Yugeun, et al. 2010. "Ulju Cheonjeon-ri gakseok-ui pyomyeon sonsang mekeonijeum haeseok," *2010-nyeon chungye jijil gwahak gisul gongdong haksul daehoe nonmunjip*.

Jeong, Byeongmo. 2010. "Jungguk, Siberia amgakhwa inmyeon-gwa Cheonjeon-ri amgakhwa inmyeon-ui dosang haeseok," *Cheonjeon-ri amgakhwa balgyeon 40-junyeon ginyeom haksul daehoe nonmunjip*.

Jeong, Dongchan. 1996. *Sarainneun sinhwa bawi geurim*, Hyean.

Jo, Cheolsu. 2000. "Jeongbo-ui balsaeng-gwa geurim munja, geurigo Ulsan amgakhwa-ui sangjing chegye," *Ulsan amgakhwa balgyeon 30-junyeon ginyeom amgakhwa gukje haksul daehoe nonmunjip*, Seoul Arts Center, Ulsan Metropolitan City.

Jo, Hongje and Mun, Jonggyu. 2010. "Daegok-cheon amgakhwa gun-ui gonghakjeok jindan-gwa bojon bangan-ui jean," *Hanguk amban gonghak hoeji 20*.

Jo, Yongjin. 2010. "Cheonjeon-ri eolgul amgakhwa-reul geurin saramdeul," *Cheonjeon-ri amgakhwa balgyeon 40-junyeon ginyeom haksul daehoe nonmunjip*.

Kim, Changho. 1995. "Ulju Cheonjeon-ri seoseok-ui haeseok munje," *Hanguk sanggosa hakbo 19*.

Kim, Eunseon. 2010. "Cheonjeon-ri amgakhwa dongmulsang-ui dosanghakjeok uimiwa yangsang," *Cheonjeon-ri amgakhwa balgyeon 40-junyeon ginyeom haksul daehoe nonmunjip*.

Kim, Hoseok. 2005. "Cheonjeon-ri amgakhwa-ui dosang haeseok," *Hanguk amgakhwa yeongu 6*.

__________. 2007. "Hanguk amgakhwa-wa bukbang asia jiyeok amgakhwa-ui johyeongjeok-in teukjing bigyo yeongu," *Jungang asia yeongu 12*.

Kim, Hyeongwon. 2010. "Cheonjeon-ri amgakhwa-ui haengnyeoldo-wa Goguryeo byeokhwa," *Cheonjeon-ri amgakhwa balgyeon 40-junyeon ginyeom haksul daehoe nonmunjip*.

Kim, Inhui. 2010. "Gihahakmun-euro bon Cheonjeon-ri amgakhwa," *Hanguk amgakhwa yeongu 14*.

Kim, Jeongbae. 2010. "Cheonjeon-ri amgakhwa-ui hanguksa-eseo-ui uiui," *Cheonjeon-ri amgakhwa balgyeon 40-junyeon ginyeom haksul daehoe nonmunjip*.

Kim, Sujin. 2000. "Ulsan amgakhwa-ui bojonmunje," *Ulsan amgakhwa balgyeon*

30-junyeon ginyeom amgakhwa gukje haksul daehoe nonmunjip, Seoul Arts Center, Ulsan Metropolitan City.

Kim, Taesik. 2005. "Jejang-uiroseoui Cheonjeon-ri seoseokgok-gwa jegwan-uiroseoui Silla wangsil-ui yeoindeul," *Hanguk amgakhwa yeongu 6.*

Kim, Wonryong. 1980. "Ulju Bangudae amgakhwa-e daehayeo," *Hanguk gogo hakbo 9.*

Kim, Yongseon. 1979. "Ulju Cheonjeon-ri seoseok myeongmun yeongu," *Yeoksa hakbo 81.*

Mun, Myeongdae. 1973. "Ulsan-ui seonsa sidae ambyeok gakhwa," *Munhwajae 7.*

_________. 2000. "Ulsan amgakhwa-ui balgyeon gyeongwi-wa yeongu seonggwa hoego," *Ulsan amgakhwa balgyeon 30-junyeon ginyeom amgakhwa gukje haksul daehoe nonmunjip*, Seoul Arts Center, Ulsan Metropolitan City.

_________. 2010. "Cheonjeon-ri amgakhwa-ui balgyeon uimiwa dosang-ui jaehaeseok," *Cheonjeon-ri amgakhwa balgyeon 40-junyeon ginyeom haksul daehoe nonmunjip*.

National Research Institute of Cultural Heritage. 2009. "Ulju Cheonjeon-ri gakseok silcheuk hwesondo pyeongga josa bogoseo," Institute of Conservation Science for Cultural Heritage, Kongju National University.

Pak, Jeonggeun. 2001. "Hanguk-ui amgakhwa jung inmulsang-e daehan goch al," *Minsokhak yeongu 9.*

_________. 2005. "Cheonjeon-ri amgakhwa-ui seongak geurim bunseok," *Hanguk amgakhwa yeongu 6.*

Pak, Yeonghui (Park, Young-hee). 1984. "Ulju Cheonjeon-ri amgakhwa-ui jejak sigie daehayeo," Master Dissertation, Ehwa Womans University.

_________. 2005. "Cheonjeon-ri amgakhwa-ui giha munyang jung mareummo kkol-ui sangjingseong-e daehan ilgochal," *Hanguk amgakhwa yeongu 6.*

Seo, Yeongdae. 2009. "Hanguk amgakhwa-ui sinanggwa uirye," *Hanguk amgakhwa yeongu 11-12.*

Seoul Arts Center and Ulsan Metropolitan City. 2000. *Ulsan amgakhwa balgyeon 30-junyeon ginyeom amgakhwa gukje haksul daehoe nonmunjip.*

Song, Gwangik. 1978. "Hanguk seonsa sidae amgakhwa-ui ilyeongu," Master Dissertation, Keimyung University.

Song, Hwaseop. 1991. "Hanguk-ui amseok gakhwa-wa geu uirye-e daehan gochal," *Hanguk sasangsa; Seoksan Han Jongman baksa hwagap ginyeom nonmunjip*, Wonkwang University Press.

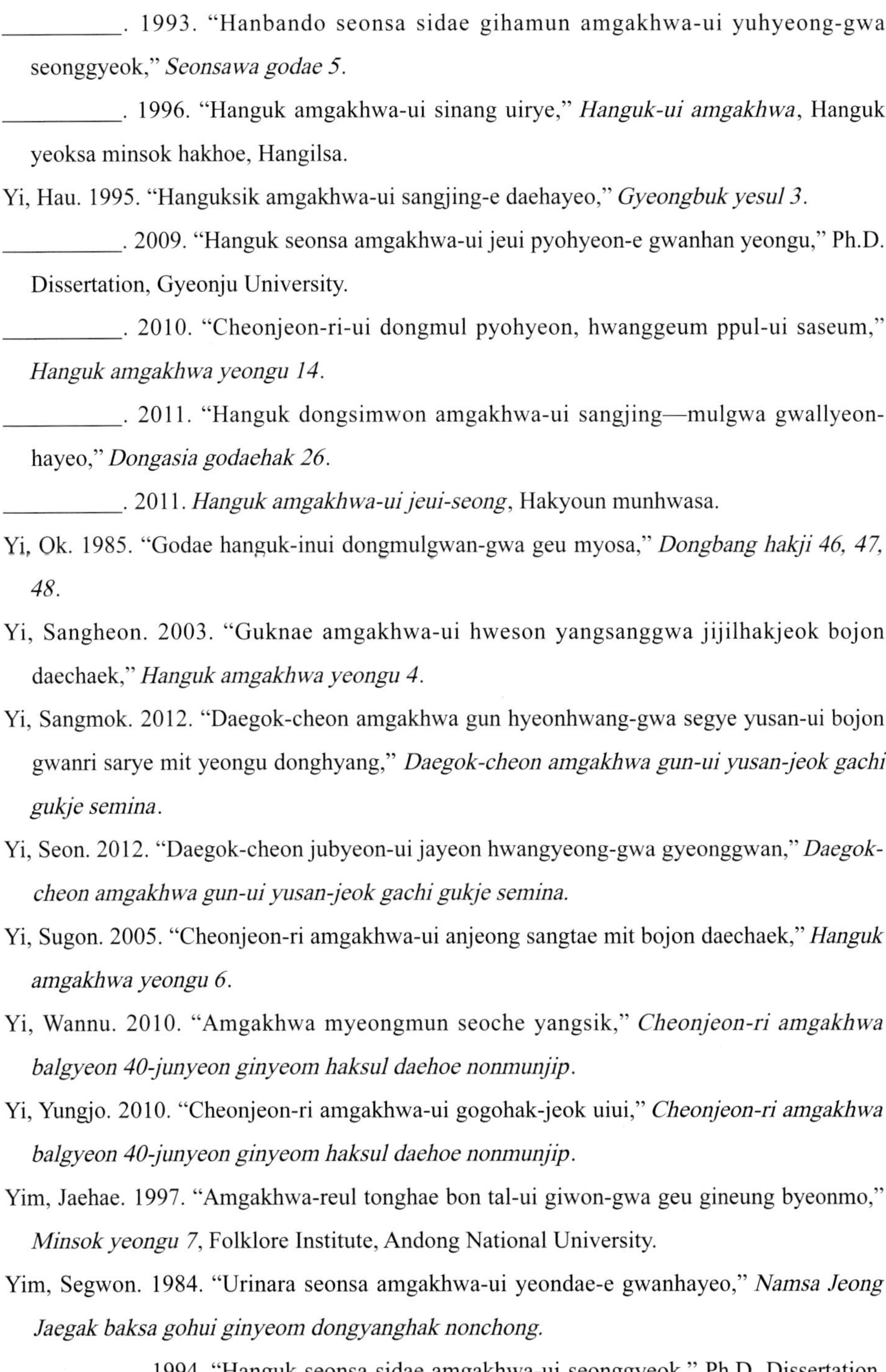

__________. 1993. “Hanbando seonsa sidae gihamun amgakhwa-ui yuhyeong-gwa seonggyeok,” *Seonsawa godae 5*.

__________. 1996. “Hanguk amgakhwa-ui sinang uirye,” *Hanguk-ui amgakhwa*, Hanguk yeoksa minsok hakhoe, Hangilsa.

Yi, Hau. 1995. “Hanguksik amgakhwa-ui sangjing-e daehayeo,” *Gyeongbuk yesul 3*.

__________. 2009. “Hanguk seonsa amgakhwa-ui jeui pyohyeon-e gwanhan yeongu,” Ph.D. Dissertation, Gyeonju University.

__________. 2010. “Cheonjeon-ri-ui dongmul pyohyeon, hwanggeum ppul-ui saseum,” *Hanguk amgakhwa yeongu 14*.

__________. 2011. “Hanguk dongsimwon amgakhwa-ui sangjing—mulgwa gwallyeon-hayeo,” *Dongasia godaehak 26*.

__________. 2011. *Hanguk amgakhwa-ui jeui-seong*, Hakyoun munhwasa.

Yi, Ok. 1985. “Godae hanguk-inui dongmulgwan-gwa geu myosa,” *Dongbang hakji 46, 47, 48*.

Yi, Sangheon. 2003. “Guknae amgakhwa-ui hweson yangsanggwa jijilhakjeok bojon daechaek,” *Hanguk amgakhwa yeongu 4*.

Yi, Sangmok. 2012. “Daegok-cheon amgakhwa gun hyeonhwang-gwa segye yusan-ui bojon gwanri sarye mit yeongu donghyang,” *Daegok-cheon amgakhwa gun-ui yusan-jeok gachi gukje semina*.

Yi, Seon. 2012. “Daegok-cheon jubyeon-ui jayeon hwangyeong-gwa gyeonggwan,” *Daegok-cheon amgakhwa gun-ui yusan-jeok gachi gukje semina*.

Yi, Sugon. 2005. “Cheonjeon-ri amgakhwa-ui anjeong sangtae mit bojon daechaek,” *Hanguk amgakhwa yeongu 6*.

Yi, Wannu. 2010. “Amgakhwa myeongmun seoche yangsik,” *Cheonjeon-ri amgakhwa balgyeon 40-junyeon ginyeom haksul daehoe nonmunjip*.

Yi, Yungjo. 2010. “Cheonjeon-ri amgakhwa-ui gogohak-jeok uiui,” *Cheonjeon-ri amgakhwa balgyeon 40-junyeon ginyeom haksul daehoe nonmunjip*.

Yim, Jaehae. 1997. “Amgakhwa-reul tonghae bon tal-ui giwon-gwa geu gineung byeonmo,” *Minsok yeongu 7*, Folklore Institute, Andong National University.

Yim, Segwon. 1984. “Urinara seonsa amgakhwa-ui yeondae-e gwanhayeo,” *Namsa Jeong Jaegak baksa gohui ginyeom dongyanghak nonchong*.

__________. 1994. “Hanguk seonsa sidae amgakhwa-ui seonggyeok,” Ph.D. Dissertation,

Dankook University.

__________. 1999. "Hanguk amgakhwa-e natanan taeyangsin sungbae," *Hanguk amgakhwa yeongu 1*.

__________. 1999. *Hanguk-ui amgakhwa*, Daewonsa.

Yun, Myeongcheol. 2010. "Ulsan Cheonjeon-ri amgakhwa-wa haeyang munhwa-ui yeongwanseong," *Hanguk amgakhwa yeongu 14*.